Financial Adulting

Take Control of Your Financial Future

Financial Adulting

Take Control of Your Financial Future

Aaron Rubin

SP Publishing
2019

Aaron Rubin
Financial Adulting
Take Control of Your Financial Future
Aaron Rubin
Copyright © 2019 by Aaron Rubin
All Rights Reserved

Art Director: Laura J. Testa-Reyes, Catalyst Creations West
First Printing 2019

Printed in the United States of America

Published in the United States of America by Aaron Rubin Publishing
ISBN-9780578469041

To my teachers: My mother and father, John Goldhammer, Dad Massoud, and Alan Werba

Table of Contents

Table of Illustrations

CHAPTER 1

Studio Living: Canned Chili Never Tasted So Good

Remember college? It was awesome, wasn't it? On most days, there was no reason to wake up before 10:00. You had maybe sixteen hours of class time, but the rest of the week was free to do whatever, whenever. Perhaps you even studied a little bit too.

Remember your first job?

My first job sucked.

Don't get me wrong—I really wanted to help the Jewish Campus Service Corps (JCSC) with their mission of creating a new culture on campus. It's just that it came at a cost for a newly graduated kid like me, trying to find a place to live in Silicon Valley.

The base salary for a JCSC Fellow was about $19,000 a year. Cost of living was adjusted for certain areas, so when I decided to take my mission to San Jose, California, I was granted an extra $3,000. That's right: I had a whopping $22,000 to live on in Silicon Valley.

I did some quick math: My car payment was $300 a month; auto insurance was $100; I spent $200 for groceries; $100 for taxes; $60 for my cell phone (god bless those Nokias). Tack on an extra $100 for gas, another $100 for incidentals, and $200 for an emergency fund. That left me with a little over $600 a month for rent and utilities in an area where the average rent at that time was $2,000 a month for a one-bedroom apartment (cue laugh track).

Perhaps in the Midwest or any other region of the United States, these numbers would have reasonably worked, but not in Silicon Valley. People were just realizing that the tech bubble had burst but had not come to grips with how bad things were about to get. Even when they had realized that the "New Economy" was just another cycle, the real estate market was un-impacted.

Lucky for me, the director of Hillel of Silicon Valley (HSV) knew a guy who knew a guy who owned a triplex house. It was a normal-sized house, three bedrooms, but the owner had divided it into three parts. One part contained the garage (converted to a room) and two of the three bedrooms. It was inhabited by a religious family of five.

On the other end was the landlord's mother, a sweet old lady.

My apartment was sandwiched between the two, a middle unit, which technically had no bedrooms. It was fifteen feet across and thirty feet deep. It had a bed and a table jiggered together with a piece of plywood and two rusty legs. But I didn't care. My rent was $500 a month, and it included utilities!

There was no oven or stove, but I was able to make some pretty serious meals using just Stagg's beef chili, curry powder, and a potato. I would eat at my desk, which was really just that table jiggered together with a piece of plywood and two rusty legs. My TV was propped up on a cardboard box, and—geez, this sounds worse when I write it out. Never mind the details. The point is it was all I needed at the time and nothing more.

I wouldn't say that I look back at that time fondly. I do admire my spartan existence and the simplicity of it all, and I appreciate all of those who choose to work in the not-for-profit sector and dedicate their lives to something bigger. I have also carried that experience with me from job to job—and I'm also still working on shedding all of the sodium that accumulated in my body from the substantial amount of canned chili that I ate.

Why did I take this job? The pay was terrible. The work, while meaningful, was not exactly stimulating. I was far removed from friends and family. I still can't say, but maybe it was the naiveté that comes with just graduating and feeling like you can change the world in a certain way. But I have no regrets. The lessons learned during that time have stayed with me all through law school, my studies to become a CPA and CFP, and even now as I sit here before you, a successful published author (LOL). My spartan existence (the spartans ate chili, I'm sure of it) showed me how to prioritize what I spent my money on, and it taught me that you can get a lot from a little.

Learning to Set Your Priorities and Say No to Yourself

A decade later I was having a conversation about careers and choices with a newly minted lawyer who was making decent money. She asked me the dreaded financial advisor question: How would I allocate her paycheck?

I dread this question because it's never an easy conversation to have with someone. Money is a personal thing, and even more so when it comes to decisions on how to spend a paycheck (as opposed to something a bit more removed and abstract, like retirement savings). This particular conversation would be especially unpleasant because my friend had quite a hill to climb financially: She'd gone to a prestigious but overpriced law school and was over $100,000 in debt from her student loans. Her husband also had $100,000 in student loan debt. They had a car payment and rent, along with other life expenses. And like most people in their demographic, they wanted the American dream: a house, savings for retirement, and money for their future children's college educations.

On top of all this, they wanted to live in the California Bay Area.

The Bay Area boasts some of the most expensive home prices in the world. In 2017, the median price of a home in San Jose finally crossed $1 million. This is over four times the average home price in the United States. A standard 20% down payment was $200,000. Even two college educated people employed full-time with high-paying jobs would struggle to save for a down payment and save for the rest of their goals.

My answer to her was simple: She needed to sacrifice something. If she wanted to save for a down payment on the house, forget about retirement, saving for college, and paying down student debt. If she was willing to sacrifice the house and rent for an indefinite period of time, then she could save more aggressively for other things. It was like a sad, weird game of whack-a-mole. Isn't adulting fun?

This response bummed her out, but there is no magic bullet. Money as an economic good is scarce; so with a limited supply, every person must deploy their resources to best match their underlying values. Do you stay in the Bay Area to be near family and friends, or do you move away to pursue other life goals? Do you decide that where you live supersedes retirement savings? These are hard decisions to make, and they cannot be made for you—hence, the reason why these conversations are uncomfortable.

My friend ended up moving out of state. She and her husband made the very tough decision that living in a place where they could afford to purchase a home and still have money for student loan debt, retirement, and college funds was more important than living near friends and family. Humans have made decisions like this for millennia. When resources are scarce, you relocate to a place where your family has the best chance to survive and thrive. Of course, it was easier for our cave-dwelling predecessors to set priorities: Make a decision or die. My friend and her husband asked themselves some tough questions, and there may have been tears and arguments, but in the end, they made a responsible choice. They may not be near their friends and family anymore, but at least now there isn't a saber-toothed tiger chasing them down (figuratively).

Building Blocks for a Secure Financial Future (Cut Out the Starbucks; You'll Survive)

Having financial security today and in the future is attainable for most of my clients, even without sacrificing everything they love. You don't have to go through martyrdom to achieve everything that is important to you (assuming you live outside the most expensive areas of the country anyway), but, nevertheless, there are some tough choices to be made.

When clients go through my financial discovery process, I look at a handful of financial indicators:

» I want to know if they have an emergency fund.
» I take a look at their 401(k)/403(b)/IRA contributions.

» I get information about their outstanding debt.

» I look at the rest of the cash they have. Having a finely balanced network of debt and savings tells me a lot about a person's financial health.

Making Sure You Have an Emergency Fund

An emergency fund is a must. This should be a cash account that goes completely untouched. Its only purpose is for use in case of unemployment or illness that prevents someone from earning their normal paycheck. Many advisors will say that an emergency fund should have a year's worth of expenses. I advise my clients to plan for six months. Either way, you can't go wrong if you are making a concerted effort to plan for an emergency.

This emergency fund is to be used in two scenarios: First, you find yourself out of a job and need to cover living expenses. Second, a truly unforeseen and horrific event occurs (roof replacement, hot water heater explodes, death or injury of someone you share expenses with).

Once you tap into this pot of money, you must make it a priority to replenish it because the next unforeseen and horrific event may be just around the corner.

Saving for Retirement ASAP

People have to rely upon their own personal savings for retirement. Gone are the days of pensions. For you millennials, a pension was savings that your employer did for you so that you could have a paycheck after retirement for the rest of your life. Federal, state, and local governments still have pensions, but don't bother asking your tech company. Also, if you are a millennial, or xennial like me, like me, you are not counting on any Social Security. The best thing to do for retirement is to start saving early. You want as many years of compounding as possible. Luckily, there are some great investment avenues to help you save for the long term.

A 401(k) is an excellent opportunity to save for the future. If your employer provides a 401(k), *take advantage of this.* You can make pre-tax contributions up to $19,000 (indexed for inflation) for 2019. When the money is taken out many years down the line, the income is then taxed at ordinary rates. If you were lucky enough to have matching contributions, it's basically free money. So if you retain nothing else from this book, let it be this: Aaron Rubin says take free money.

An employee would be crazy not to participate. Again, it's free money (do I have your attention yet?). Many plans offer a safe harbor match where the employer adds to an employee's account dollar for dollar up to 3% of compensation. Any amount above 3% is matched 50 cents on the dollar up to 5%. If an employee doesn't at least do 3%, they are missing out on an immediate 100% rate of return. Don't be the person who celebrates your seventieth birthday at work, wishing you had upped your 401(k) contribution forty years earlier to 3%.

Since some companies do not offer a 401(k) plan, you may need to save for retirement in an Individual Retirement Account (IRA). An IRA is similar to a 401(k) in tax treatment. However, instead of an $19,000 limitation, there is an annual $5,000 limitation for those under age 50 and $6,000 for those aged 50 or older. What's more, there are income limitations, and you must have earned income to save inside of an IRA.

Another amazing investment avenue is the Roth 401(k). Similar to a traditional 401(k), a Roth 401(k) allows a person to put in after-tax dollars and take out the money tax-free later on. With a Roth, you can have the income included for income tax purposes in the current year, but the growth of your invested money will all come out tax free at the end. This is a Gen Yer's dream. Later on in life, most Gen Yers will be in a higher tax bracket, even when retired, as opposed to in their youth. This means that money went in relatively inexpensively and comes out when tax rate is higher. You can also save inside of a Roth IRA, which is very similar to a Roth 401(k), but be aware of income limitations. Again, those under age 50 are limited to $5,000 per year, and $6,000 for those aged 50 or older.

If this is confusing to you, do not get discouraged. Choosing one over the other is not going to result in a mistake of epic proportions that seriously impacts your retirement. However, not investing money in a 401(k) of some kind will lead to disaster. Get in early, and let the power of compounding interest carry you to a possible, if not comfortable, retirement.

Debt and Short-Term Savings

Credit cards are evil. They (or their marketing and sales departments) have, in a relatively short period of time, changed a nation's thinking about how to leverage debt to your advantage and how to differentiate between needs and wants. How do you as a consumer determine the best method to purchase, say, a new television? Do you save responsibly, then spend it all in one fell swoop? Or do you buy it now on credit and pay it off with no additional financial cost? Either way, you get a TV and money is spent (whether it was saved or borrowed), but determining the smart way to spend versus save can be confusing.

From the time we are in college until long after we've died, we are inundated with credit card offers. I have one friend who even managed to get a credit card for his dog. Truth be told, debt is a fascinating tool. Clearly, without debt and credit, many businesses would never make it off the ground, and most people (especially in California) would not own homes. However, debt used for consumer goods is responsible for the downfall of millions of Americans. If consumer debt hasn't negatively impacted you, chances are it's impacted someone close to you.

I knew lots of kids in college who got hooked early. By the time they were sophomores, they had minimum payments due on their credit cards that forced them to have to work at a time when they should have been focused on their education. My own grandmother was a notorious abuser of credit cards, and she financed all sorts of trips and shopping sprees with no real plan on how to pay for them afterward. With interest rates as high as 20% and finance charges, it takes many years to pay off a card with minimum payments.

Debt should be a tool. If you're thinking responsibly, debt should be placed in the "investment" category. Debt should really be meant as a way to obtain assets used for income-producing purposes, or long-term investment, and not to augment current spending.

Using debt (also called leverage) to purchase a business or start a business is important to the business cycle process. Similarly, using debt to finance a house purchase is also a wise use. After all, for most Americans, their biggest asset is going to be their personal residence. College or trade school debt has a similar story: It is an asset that will be used to make more money in the future. On its face, education is a wise investment. Whether or not paying $50,000 a year for a political science degree from Stanford as opposed to $20,000 at San Jose State University is a wise decision is another debate entirely.

What is not an appropriate use of debt? Everything else: televisions, high-end clothing, luxury cars, etc. These things do not produce income, depreciate close to 100% over time, and must be replaced at least every ten years or less. Am I guilty of inappropriately using debt? Absolutely.

So, how are we supposed to afford things like fancy cars and televisions? The answer is savings. A person's savings is the best way to accumulate the cash needed for noninvestment purchases. How badly do you want that $35,000 BMW 3 Series? If you want it in the next twelve months and can save $2,916.66 each month, then it's all yours. In the meantime, a new Ford Fiesta, which costs around $14,000 will do. Make sure you know the financing details: 0% is best, but try not to go above 1.9%. Or try used cars and let someone else pay for most of the depreciation up front.

Budgeting for Retirement: Tilting at Windmills

No one is born knowing how to save for retirement. At best, we pick up information along the way, educating ourselves by reading books (like this one), taking courses, and talking to financial professionals. At worst, we learn from our terrible mistakes. The first step of any rehab program is to admit you have a problem. But it's okay because, if you're reading this book, you are already past this first step of awareness and can skip right to the good stuff: budgeting.

Tracking personal spending is foundational to creating a budget. It provides a baseline understanding of your monthly spend on things that don't change, such as rent, phone, loans, and various subscriptions (Netflix, cable, etc.). For things like groceries and clothing, you'll want three months of data to figure out a monthly average. Electric and water bills should also be averaged, but the bills need to be over a yearlong period since electricity use peaks in the summer and natural gas use is more in the winter. Thankfully, this is relatively easy to calculate, as most utilities have online platforms and prior usage data that is easily accessible.

The trickier part is accounting for the random expenditures. In my house, there is always that unexpected event that occurs that we usually call a "one-off." That one-off ranges from a car repair to a veterinary bill to a wedding gift for a close friend. Yet, despite it being a supposed one-off, it seems that every quarter a one-off happens (which means I should call them four-offs). One-offs are an important part of creating a functional budget

You'll want to sort every expenditure into a category —the more specific, the better. Too often when we do budgets, the tendency is to lump all discretionary spending into entertainment. This renders a budget largely useless. Your entertainment category should have subcategories, such as dining out, movies, iTunes purchases, and nights out at the bars where you may or may not have lost your keys and debit card and woken up with a shattered phone. You can just shorten that to "Saturday nights" if you like. Being able to know where your money goes is empowering because it allows you to effect change that you can readily track.

Congrats, you now know where your money is going. At this point, you should be able to reduce expenses to at least have a balanced budget—you can choose to survive or thrive. If the desire is to thrive rather than just survive, forcing additional changes to your behavior may allow you to save money and start to build a nest egg or a more secure emergency fund. If, at age twenty-five, you can cut your Starbucks habit in half and instead put $65 per month in a Roth 401(k), after 40 years you'll have almost $100,000 tax-free, assuming a conservative 5% rate of return. Ask anyone who's done this, and they'll swear that tall vanilla latte tastes way better post-retirement.

Here is a sample annual budget for the emerging professional:

Income

Wages	60,000
Expenses	
401(k)	6,000
Taxes	14,000
Rent	15,500
Car payment	4,300
Auto insurance	1,300
Renter's insurance	600
Cell phone	1,000
Utilities	3,800
Food	2,400
Booze	1,000
Emergency fund	4,000
Netflix (and chill?)	120
Hulu (Plus?)	150

Vacation	2,000
Gifts	600
Eating out	2,000
iTunes	500
Starbucks	330
Excess	400

A budget should be reviewed on an annual basis.

Budgeting for the Unknown

However, a current budget is just the start of the exercise. Your life (and, in turn, your budget) will not remain the same. If you are in your mid-twenties, chances are you don't have kids. There is nothing more expensive in this universe than a human child. You may want to get married. Or buy a house, or continue your education, or foster puppies, or buy a guava plantation—or all those things. Whatever your dreams for the future are, you'll need to budget accordingly to help yourself achieve those dreams.

The second part of this introspective experiment is trying to budget for the unknown. To do that, you are going to need to make some sweeping assumptions about where your life is headed. You have to start somewhere. If you don't know much about raising a child or how much a house costs, ask a friend and be sure to bring beer because you both are going to need it.

Once you've listed out a few big-picture dreams and rough costs associated with them, take your current budget and add in everything that is going to come later on. Add in college savings, landscaping, mortgage payments, increased everyday living expenses, day care, and family vacations. Once you have all of that in and are sufficiently overwhelmed, you need to figure out how short you are on your monthly income. Now, we whittle away at that amount in order to make your dreams a reality.

That shortage can be made up several ways. First, you will likely continue to make more money. Take into account what you're making now, what the income ceiling is in your industry, and your likelihood of moving up. It won't be perfect, but it will further reduce the gap in your budget and get you closer to achieving your long-term goals. (I told you this would require some imagination and assumptions.)

You can also sacrifice some expenses. If you really want that guava plantation, limit yourself to cash-only nights at the bars, cancel one of your TV subscriptions, or skip the expensive haircut. Take the amount saved and deduct it from the gap in your budget.

Second, you will likely be married or have a domestic partner, and that person has an income to contribute to your household that will only further assist in attaining your goals, which are now likely shared goals—hence, the reason an annual review is recommended. This means that if you marry a high-power Google executive, you're in better shape than if you marry an aspiring death metal guitar player (#goalsdigger). Not that I'm recommending one over the other—marry who you love—but understand there are financial consequences.

So you marry the death metal guitar player, and he or she can rock some gnarly chords, but their income consists of minimal booking fees and bad IPAs. When reexamining that budget, you are going to have to make a sacrifice somewhere else. Perhaps you live in a very expensive area. Nearly every job can be done in a different part of the country, although there are exceptions. Certain cities are high-tech hubs that have a large demand for engineers and IP lawyers. Oil and gas tycoons and their attorneys typically find themselves in Texas, Oklahoma, or the Dakotas. If you are an insurance adjuster, you can do that anywhere; same with being a death metal guitar player.

Third, you may stand to inherit a lot of money. If this is the case, then worrying about retirement is not as pressing. Of course, if your parents live into their late nineties, you may be working well into your seventies, but so long as you are willing to hold out, time remains undefeated. Of course, your parents may spend all of your inheritance without your permission, in which case the plan falls apart. So it's probably best to have a contingency plan.

Check, Please!

While Gen Y can expect to face some hard financial challenges the first half of this century, these obstacles are not insurmountable. By following some simple rules about allocating income, Gen Y can come into the second half of the century well prepared for what lies ahead.

Following are five steps that a modern millennial can take right now that will improve your financial well-being while living in that studio apartment:

1. **Never forget.** You lived like a pauper at one point; don't let lifestyle creep happen to you. Taking canned chili off the menu does not mean you have to substitute it with filet mignon.

2. **Start the cash lifestyle early.** Credit card companies and retail outlets are always enticing you to buy up and to buy on credit. This is how financial disaster occurs. Debt should be used for appreciating and income-producing assets only.

3. **Just say yes...to delayed gratification.** If you hear in your head "I can splurge," take your wallet and throw it into the nearest body of water. Better yet, write the idea down, put it in an envelope, sleep with it under your pillow, and see if it's still a good idea in the morning.

4. **Get that 401(k) going.** The earlier you save, the more you'll have in retirement. By starting to save a few hundred dollars a month in your twenties, you can avoid having to scramble in your fifties. Use the Roth 401(k) option, if available, and your income is relatively low. Sometimes you can contribute to a 401(k) and a Roth IRA, but there are limitations based upon income.

5. **Build an emergency fund.** You need an emergency fund. You need an emergency fund. You need an emergency fund. This is important, not a typo. Have at least six months' cash liquid and ready to go.

CHAPTER 2
Between Death and Taxes, Choose Death

In 2003, when I went to law school, I wanted to be a tax attorney. (I don't know what's wrong with me, but all CPAs have a neurological dysfunction of some sort, and tax is mine.) I took as many tax classes as I could find and volunteered on weekends as a tax preparer for the poor.

Prior to volunteering at the tax center, I had never done a single tax return. In essence, I was like a dental student practicing my trade. I learned a lot—some about tax preparation, but mostly about people. Every client who came through the door was putting complete trust in me to comply with their legal obligation to file income tax returns and to access their tax benefits.

My task was to answer the questions of if and/or how much they owed. Those answers could ruin their day, week, month, or year. We were both muddling our way through a Byzantine system where a privileged few could write the rules. Only the supremely educated could understand those rules, and only the wealthy could pay for that advice. The poor working schlubs were stuck with half-bright law students.

As I transitioned into public accounting, the distance between those doing the taxing and the taxed became more and more apparent. The system is designed so that almost nobody can understand it. Some politicians claim they want equity; some desire simplicity. Yet, despite all of the rhetoric, we are no closer to either of those ideals. All we have is the thief in the night known as the Internal Revenue Code (IRC).

While you should always be respectful to anyone working in the Internal Revenue Service (IRS) the IRS, as an institution is not your friend. The tax code is trying to take your money, and the IRS enforces that code. Be combative in preparing your return. Come in with the mind-set that Form 1040 is a contest between you and the government over who gets to keep your money. In this chapter, I'll show you how to break down the tax code and make the system work for you as much as possible.

Income: Show Me the Money! (No Matter Where It Came From!)

The tax code can be generally broken down into three different pieces:

» Income
» Deductions
» Credits

Income may seem like a straightforward concept, but in reality, it is quite complex. The tax code defines "income" as all money received from whatever source derived. Did your grandmother leave you her IRA when she passed away? Yup, that's taxable income.

When we are young and our government-defined "income" is simpler and more streamlined (meaning you only earn money from your job, maybe a small investment here or there), filing taxes is pretty simple, and there's not much that can be done to influence what you report on your tax forms. However, as we get older and our finances become more complex (money coming in from your job, stock options, more investments across many asset classes, addition of dependents), that's when we can start thinking about a concept called shifting income.

Shifting income basically means we can get creative with how income is reported to the IRS in order to get the best outcome possible. Don't think of it as cheating (since it's perfectly legal), but rather gaming the system. We are engaging in arbitrage: moving income to a different person or tax year to get the best rates. This is also why it's helpful to have a professional help you with your taxes.

Timing Is Everything: Getting the Best Tax Rate

Postponement of recognition is one way to shift income, but it's a bit easier said than done, and it has its own set of risks. The main way most people postpone income is by choosing when to recognize gains and losses in investments. The world of capital gains is generally divided among two different types (for more exotic investments there are more, but let's keep it to the vast majority): short-term and long-term gains.

A *short-term capital gain* is gain on an investment that you've had for one year or less.. A long-term capital gain is one which you've had for more than one year. The taxation difference is important: For long-term gains, the current rate of taxation is less. That means you are disincentivized from trying to cash in on investments made less than a year ago—you certainly can, but if you do, you'll pay more in taxes to the government. Those who are in the 12% bracket or below pay 0%, those above the 12% bracket but below the 35% rate pay 15%, and those in the highest bracket pay 20%. Holding on to an asset to receive long-term gain treatment has to be a factor in a decision to sell.

The flip side of that is recognizing losses. At the end of a year when you had short-term capital gains, it's important to try to offset those gains with losses so as not to be taxed at ordinary rates. Long-term losses can offset short-term gains, as long as they are first used to offset the long-term gains. Taking an inventory of the type of income you have and the timing makes end-of-year decisions crucial.

If you have stock options, there is also a way to creatively report earnings. While most people working in the high-tech industry receive restricted stock units (RSUs), there are still a large amount of incentive stock options (ISOs) and non-qualified stock options (NQSOs) floating around. Understanding how to time these transactions can make a huge difference in taxes.

RSUs are pretty cut-and-dry. They are taxed on the date received and at fair market value. In addition, the company that issued the RSUs is required to do withholding as well. There isn't much tax strategy involved. When the stock vests, sell. Whether your company gives you RSUs or you purchase on the open market, you receive no economic or tax advantage from holding the granted shares.

NQSOs are a bit more interesting. With NQSOs, the person is taxed at the bargain they received when purchased. The "bargain" is defined as the current fair market value less the amount you paid for the stock. That bargain is taxed at ordinary rates. Any gain after exercising those options is going to be capital. Hold for a year, and you can get long-term capital gains. Of course, you will be taking market risk during that time, so be careful.

ISOs have the biggest tax potential. With an ISO, a taxpayer buys the stock for a bargain. That bargain is a preference item for the alternative minimum tax (AMT), which will be discussed later on. Basically, AMT taxes you on the paper gain when you purchase the stock. If the taxpayer holds the stock for a year, the original bargain and any additional gain will be taxed at preferential rates. By holding for a year, a taxpayer can get a major break on their tax bill. Remember, you are still taking on market risk as you try to hold for a year!

Arbitrage, My Favorite French word

Another way to avoid taxes is through *arbitrage*, which is shifting income from a high-income taxpayer to a low-income taxpayer. The taxpayer may be in a high bracket, but their kids or grandkids have no tax at all since they have no income. Kids are usually key to this strategy, and, again, yes, this is legal. The idea is that if a parent can spin off an asset that will sell at a gain to a child who has no income, they'll get lower tax rates. However, Congress has thought of this and implemented a tax regime for minors called "Kiddie Tax."

With Kiddie Tax, the first $1,050 (indexed for inflation) of investment income earned by a child is tax-free, the next $1,050 is taxed at the child's rate, and anything above that is taxed at the parent's rate. This means if you give a child $2,200 of income they pay zero tax, but every dollar above $2,200 gets taxed at trust tax rates. Trust tax brackets are brutal and reach the 37% bracket with income that exceeds $12,500. Similarly, the 20% bracket for long-term capital gains also starts at $12,500. To make matters worse, a child is anyone below the age of eighteen, or a full-time student under age twenty-four who does not provide more than half of their own support.

Don't worry, all is not lost. When the child reaches age twenty four, all bets are off. No longer subject to Kiddie Tax, parents can then shift high-income producing investments and low-basis investments to their kids. Most kids coming out of college don't have much and are still in super low tax brackets. If you've been meaning to sell that Apple stock you bought in the 1980s but couldn't bring yourself to pay the tax, make some Apple stock your child's graduation gift. (Note: If giving large sums, over $15,000 per year indexed for inflation, a parent needs to be aware of gift tax requirements and special gift tax filings.)

Deductions: Itemizing Your Life

Deductions are more easily understood. They are spelled out throughout the tax code. Like the income side, they are subject to abuse, misinterpretation, and lengthy court battles.

While corporations call the shots in Congress and can get special carve-outs, we individuals need to take the crumbs we are given. There are two ways a taxpayer can go: standard deduction or itemized deduction. The *standard deduction* is a sum that is deducted from income. That deduction can vary depending on filing status (married filing joint, single, head of household, etc.).

Because the number is indexed for inflation every year, it tends to go up. Generally, if you don't have a mortgage, don't pay a lot in state income taxes, or don't have very large medical bills, you take the standard deduction.

Itemizing is much more fun because it allows for a certain amount of creativity. The most important deduction in our tax code is the home mortgage interest deduction. When a taxpayer purchases a personal residence (or first vacation home), the mortgage is fully deductible as long as the balance on the mortgage does not exceed $750,000, which may sound like a lot of room, but that's not the case for homes in California and New York City.

With the Tax Cut and Jobs Act of 2017 (TCJA), itemizing isn't necessary for many people. This is mainly due to the increase in the standard deduction, which in 2019 is $12,200 for single taxpayers and $24,400 for those married filing jointly (indexed for inflation).

The *state income tax deduction* is also commonly used. For those in high state income tax jurisdictions, this deduction may get you close to the itemizing deduction threshold. With the TCJA, this deduction is now combined with real estate and personal property taxes and limited to $10,000.

The *real estate tax deduction* is fairly straightforward. What you pay to your local tax collector for any property owned is deductible. This is true for any property, including vacation homes and time shares. Remember, if your real estate deduction and state income tax deduction exceed $10,000 combined, you will lose anything above that amount.

The *medical deduction* is also a complicated deduction that may seem simple. The formula involves taking the taxpayer's adjusted gross income (AGI) and multiplying by 10%. Medical bills are added together, and the taxpayer deducts what is in excess of 10% AGI.

What gets interesting is deciding what qualifies as a medical expense. Generally, it's anything "medically necessary." You can imagine the obvious ones: co-pays, co-insurance, dental work, eye doctor, etc. But "medically necessary" also includes long-term care insurance, Medicare and supplemental premiums, as well as COBRA medical premiums.

Finally, the *charitable deduction* is common among taxpayers. The charitable deduction applies to both cash and non-cash gifts. With both types, a taxpayer needs contemporaneous documentation. This means that the charity, within a reasonable period of time, needs to acknowledge the gifts received. If you want to donate long-term highly appreciated stock, that's a fantastic idea! You don't have to recognize the gain, and you get a deduction. (Be sure to ask a qualified preparer about the deduction limitations of appreciated assets.)

Give Me Some Credit!

Credits are a direct offset of tax. One famous credit is the *Child Care Tax Credit*. This allows parents to take a percentage of expenses used for child care, and directly offset tax liability. A lot of high-tech companies use the *Research and Development Tax Credit*, which lets them use a percentage of R&D expenses to directly offset tax liability. Credits are applied after the tax is calculated; thus, they are a dollar-for-dollar reduction of tax.

Some credits can be quite large. The *Adoption Tax Credit*, which helps taxpayers pay for the costs of a legal adoption, is over $13,840 (indexed for inflation). The *Residential Efficient Energy Credit* is 10% of the cost of energy efficient improvements up to $500. Such improvements include windows, insulation, and HVAC systems.

Many credits phase out at certain income levels. The *Lifetime Learning Credit* gives people a 20% credit on the first $10,000 of education spent in a year. However, for married couples filing jointly, once their AGI goes over $130,000 they are phased out of the credit entirely.

Aside from phase-outs, some credits are refundable, while others are non-refundable. Refundable credits are those that taxpayers receive regardless of whether or not they actually owe any tax. A non-refundable credit means that if you don't owe any tax, you can't use the credit. The *Earned Income Credit* for low-income families is an example of a refundable credit, while the *Lifetime Learning Credit* is not.

AMT: The Dirtiest Three-Letter Acronym

How do you know that you've made it? You start paying alternative minimum tax (AMT). AMT is a separate system of taxation from the normal tax regime. Sure, you start with your regular taxable income, but certain adjustments and preferences are added back. Once AMT is calculated, the taxpayer is forced to pay the greater of AMT or regular tax.

Items that may not count as income in regular tax may be income in AMT. The most notable is gains from the exercise of incentive stock options (ISOs). Normally, the bargain a taxpayer receives from purchasing (not even selling!) company stock at a discount is not taxed. However, under AMT it is taxed. This can get someone in a lot of trouble if they buy the stock, pay the tax on the AMT, and then the price falls significantly. They may owe more in tax than the stock is worth! Don't laugh, it happened to a lot of high-tech workers back in the early 2000s.

The calculation is complex, but can be broken down. Everything starts with taxable income. From there AMT adds a bunch of deductions back (called *adjustments*), and some phantom income (called *preferences*). This yields your AMT Income. Then your AMT income given a sizeable exemption ($111,700 in 2018 (indexed for inflation) for married filing joint).

After you get your taxable AMT income, then you apply the AMT tax rates which vary between 26% and 28%. When income gets high enough, the AMT exemption itself gets phased out. Even some of the credits under regular tax are not applicable to AMT! The super-rich don't pay AMT, mainly because more of their income is taxed at 37%, which is higher than the AMT rate of 28%.

With the TCJA, fewer people will now be subject to the AMT. First, with the reduction of state and local income tax deduction to $10,000, a major add-back for AMT is now greatly reduced. Second, for those making less than $1 million, the AMT exemption is no longer phased out as easily. Under prior law, taxpayers started being phased out of the AMT exemption starting at $160,900.

A Word to My Small Business Owners

Owning a small business, whether it be contracting or a more elaborate operation, affords the taxpayer a lot of tax opportunities. Here's the thing: The IRS knows this too. The IRS is also severely understaffed, and so long as you don't go too crazy, your chances of being audited are quite slim. The trick, as with everything in life, is moderation. Pigs get fat; hogs get slaughtered.

All of that being said, don't do anything illegal.

Do push the envelope.

Every business owner needs to be aware of Section 179. Section 179 allows taxpayers to effectively expense items that are usually depreciable. Nearly everything purchased that has a useful life has to be depreciated over a term of years predefined by the IRS. Computers are depreciated over five years, office furniture over seven. This means the recovery of the expense has to be drawn out. With Section 179 a taxpayer can deduct it in the first year. As you get bigger and buy more assets, it is possible to hit a cap on 179 deductions. (TCJA has increased that cap significantly.)

Many of you are now licking your chops or getting ready to fire your tax preparer because they didn't take 179 deductions. However, not all assets are eligible. First, it can be newly acquired or used property. Prior to 2018, only new assets were eligible for 179. Second, only certain types of property are eligible. Purchasing a piece of real estate does not entitle a person to "179" their house. There are other restrictions and limitations as well. Consult your qualified tax preparer because this book is not a treatise on tax law.

Because the tax code is an ever-changing document, Congress will occasionally write goodies into the code. One such goodie that appears off and on is something called bonus depreciation or cost recovery. With bonus depreciation, the taxpayer gets to take 50% depreciation on a given new asset in the first year. However, some years it's in the tax code, some years not. You can't double-dip into 179 either.

Another overlooked and misunderstood deduction is the home office deduction. To use this deduction, your primary place of business has to be your home. Do you commute to an office every day? This deduction doesn't apply to you. Moreover, to take the deduction, the space used for work must be exclusively used for work. No storing the kids' toys in your office, and the kitchen table, almost by definition, doesn't count.

If you are not one to take out your measuring tape and parse through every bill you have, the simplified method may be the better way to go. Under the simplified method, you can deduct $5 per square foot without having to justify the expense with any records. However, you can't use the simplified method if you have more than 300 square feet of home office space.

Once you have a space in your house specifically set up for use as the principle place of business, now the fun begins. Take out your tape measure and find out how many square feet your office is. Divide that number by the total square footage of the home. That percentage is your new favorite number.

You are going to apply that percentage to nearly everything in your life. Electric, gas, garbage, phone, mortgage interest, property tax, cable, and Internet. You will depreciate this percentage of your home as well. Keep in mind this will make the taxes upon selling your house more complicated, but that is mañana. And as University of Illinois College of Law Professor Richard Kaplan says: "Mañana es mañana, and we live for today." Also, be prepared for an audit. Home office deductions are seriously scrutinized, so make sure that you are following all of the rules and have documentation.

The other obstacle small business owners have to look out for is hiring employees versus independent contractors. I know a lot of small business owners, and their favorite thing to do is "1099" people that work for them, which means they aren't responsible for the person's payroll taxes and don't have to provide benefits. Form 1099 is the miscellaneous income form. It's used to report income that is not wages (which are reported on Form W-2). Income listed on Form 1099 is typically self-employment income, which means the contractor pays payroll tax on their own tax return on Schedule SE. They also don't have to receive health care or retirement benefits.

For those on a shoestring budget, pushing these expenses to the employee is very appealing. However, there have been many actions taken against employers who abuse this tool. The most popular reason for being snagged as failing to pay payroll tax is pissed-off employees. Sometimes contractors have to be fired or even laid off. Those people are going to turn around and try to collect unemployment.

However, for 1099 contractors, they haven't paid into unemployment, and when they are told they aren't eligible they get angry. They then tell the relevant state agency that they really were employees and the employer should have been paying in. This launches an investigation, the Feds get called in, and now your small business owner really has some problems on their hands. God forbid you have a workers' comp problem because that gets nasty.

The trick behind keeping your employees as independent contractors is by being careful with how much control you exercise. There is a series of tests that helps determine if you really have employees versus independent contractors.

First, you look at the amount of control that the employer has in how the worker does their job; the more oversight, the more the person looks like an employee. There is also a financial aspect, such as how the worker is paid, and if the employer provides the tools for the job. Finally, there is the relationship itself: are there retirement benefits, are there contracts, and is there an ongoing indefinite relationship? In trying to figure out where a particular business falls, it is important to find a licensed attorney to analyze your particular situation.

A Word to My Rental Real Estate Owners

I know you love real estate. If you live in California, you REALLY love real estate. The problem is that love makes you do crazy things. At this point, preparing your own tax return when you own rental real estate falls under the "crazy things" category. Don't worry; it's not your fault. It's a confluence of events: The tax laws changed significantly, and real estate, especially in certain areas of the country, has rocketed upward.

The main issue is what is called the "Repair Regs." Up until 2014, rental real estate just wasn't that complicated. The line between expense and depreciation was blurry around the edges, but most took a SWAG (Scientific Wild-Ass Guess), and it worked out. The tax landscape is now completely different and way more complicated. Find a competent professional to do it for you.

I also want to dispel a common misconception that once you pay off a mortgage, you should go out and buy another property using a mortgage on your personal residence for tax purposes. First of all, the last two years of payments on a mortgage are nearly entirely principal, so you weren't getting much of a deduction anyway. You also need to know that if you create a loss on a rental property, you are limited on the amount of deductible loss. Once a taxpayer's AGI (single or married filing jointly) exceeds $100,000, the deductibility begins to phase out, and once over $150,000, the loss is not deductible. Otherwise, the losses are disallowed, carried forward, and are only reinstated once you have passive income (you have another property producing rental income) or you dispose of the property.

For more on real estate as investments, see Chapter 6.

Check, Please!

Tax is an important consideration for all employees and employers. When we have our first jobs, we tend to focus on gross pay and not net pay. Most people don't itemize for the first few years of their career, but as life gets complicated—house, spouse, kids—taxes get more complicated as well.

By focusing on five goals, modern millennials can make informed decisions that put the most money into their pockets:

1. **Withhold what you need to—if you constantly get big tax refunds from the government, you're losing the battle.** A refund is a free loan you gave the government. True, for some it is a forced savings account, but it's a poor use of money

   You want to withhold enough such that you owe $500 or less to the Feds. This takes some tinkering.

2. **Remember the Big Five deductions—mortgage, state income/sales taxes, property tax, medical, and charity—but be aware that the TCJA has severe limitations starting in 2018.** Focus on those. The other deductions will lower your taxes, but work on what nets you the biggest bang for your buck.

3. **Take your credits.** Credits are dollar-for-dollar reductions of tax liability. Spend some time at the end of the year and think about what major cash outlays you've had, such as improvements to your house or purchase of a car, and then Google possible credits. Better yet, hire a tax preparer and leave no stone unturned.

4. **Don't be shy; business owners have great opportunities when it comes to tax planning.** Maximize your deductions by being aggressive. But don't get greedy or you may find yourself in an orange jumpsuit. Regardless of what Netflix says, orange is not the new black.

5. **Get help.** You don't know everything, and that's okay. You need to know when you're in over your head. Rental properties, multi-state tax returns, stock options, flow through income, and more complicated business transactions are great indicators that it is time to get some help or at least a second opinion.

CHAPTER 3

Overcoming the Greatest Investment Obstacle: You

The Death of Superman...and My Bar Mitzvah Money

The first stock I ever owned was Wm. Wrigley Jr. Company. I received 20 shares from my uncle for my Bar Mitzvah. Everyone in my family considered my uncle to be a stock whiz, whatever that meant. Nevertheless, I was fascinated by the idea that I now owned a piece of a corporation and that the value would rise and fall. I was even inquisitive enough to open an annual report. Of course, I had no idea what I was looking at, so my attentiveness soon faded.

However, I kept returning to learn more. If my uncle could (presumably) make a lot of money in the stock market, then I could (presumably) do the same. A 13-year-old kid has dreams; it comes with the territory. A Super Nintendo console, new Huffy bike, Cal Ripken's rookie baseball card...I desperately wanted to have money to spend on things that were important to me. Of course, there were no jobs in my hometown available for 13-year-olds, so it seemed at the time that my only option for making money was to learn about investing.

In addition to my 20 shares of Wrigley in hand, I had a couple hundred bucks in my bank account—it was a start. I began researching what stocks to buy. Seventh graders typically aren't poring over the Motley Fool (1993 was a bad year for web research) tracking companies, valuations, and dividends, so I was limited to the only two things I really knew: baseball cards and comic books.

The two big baseball card makers at the time were Topps and Upper Deck. They were privately held, so I could not invest in those companies. This left comic books. My preferred publishers were Marvel and Image. (I was never a big DC Comics fan, but I made an exception when it came to the "Death of Superman" issue.) Image was privately owned as well, so Marvel it was. I did not know much about the company itself, but I did know that a large portion (read: all) of my allowance contributed to their bottom line every week.

I wasn't alone. In the early 1990s, comic book collecting was having a renaissance. Comic book "clubs" were formed, and you could pretty much guarantee that if you weren't part of one, you wouldn't get the next hot book you wanted. Part of the fervor was driven by baseball card collectors from a decade earlier. Many were still scarred from learning that they could have been millionaires, if only their mothers hadn't thrown out their baseball card collections during a cleaning binge. They weren't going to lose out again. As a result, speculators started sucking up all the comic books they could. And as with baseball card collecting before it, demand outpaced supply, and soon comic book companies wised up and began charging more for limited edition collector's cards, foil overlays, and other such gimmicks. Being a fan became difficult because each week brought with it a new special release at a higher price.

However, becoming an investor in the industry became an easy choice. From my perspective, a comic book company was the best investment ever. They set their price at whatever they wanted, and people stood in line to buy it. How could a company ever lose money if it could arbitrarily crank up their revenue on demand? It seemed foolproof. On top of this, Marvel's annual reports were collector's items in their own right. The company would style the first pages of the report just like a comic book, and they would illustrate, ink, and color the reports as such. It was actually a really fun thing to receive in the mail and a perfect first foray into learning how to read these typically dry, data-heavy documents. But what made me most excited about investing in Marvel was that they had just announced a stock split and however many shares I owned would soon be doubled. In my mind, that meant my investment would now grow twice as fast. Now I was in a race against time to acquire those shares before the split date.

Buying, of course, was a completely separate matter. I could not find anybody willing to help me make the purchase. There was no online trading at that time, and I only wanted 20 shares, which amounted to around $800. At that time, a broker wouldn't look at you unless you wanted a round lot (100 shares). I did not have the money for 100 shares. Enter my uncle to save the day. He called in a favor to his broker, who was able to issue me 20 shares in certificate form. Those 20 shares would soon be 40, and more shares meant more profit. Not all heroes wear capes.

So here I was, thirteen years old and having just made my first stock market investment in Marvel, a cool company that, according to my research, seemed like the perfect bet. Imagine my surprise when the value of the shares tanked after the stock split. In the ensuing three years, the stock price continued to flounder until the company eventually filed bankruptcy in 1996. I had only received two of those famous illustrated, inked, and colorized year-end reports. I was crestfallen—this was sadder than "Death of Superman." Far from making me wealthy, my first dip of the toe into the stock market taught me an incredibly valuable lesson: The stock market is a risky place. This lesson has arguably paid far more dividends in the long run than Marvel could have.

In this chapter, we explore how being human also makes us bad investors. We'll also discuss ways that we can overcome our biases and flesh out some different options that Wall Street has to offer.

When It Comes to Investing, Your Brain Can Be Your Own Worst Enemy

When I tell people that I am a wealth manager, I am typically met with one of two questions:

1. Where is the market going?

2. What do you think about [insert name of hot stock at the time]?

The correct answer to both of these questions is I don't know. If I knew, I wouldn't be talking to you about my job as a wealth manager. I'd have my own island in the Caribbean.

The truth is, I have no special insights into how the market will move in the future—because nobody knows how the market will move in the future. Anybody who claims to know where the market is going with any confidence is a charlatan of the highest order. In fact, the vast majority of managers in U.S. stocks (90%!) failed to outperform the S&P 1500 between 2008 and 2017. Let that sink in for a moment. These are the Harvard MBAs of the world. They eat, breathe, and live finance and research. Their livelihood and pay depends on their portfolio performance. Yet with all the incentives and education, their stock picking is still most likely going to miss the mark. Despite these facts, we continue to regard investment professionals as the gatekeepers to financial gains and freedom.

In the face of both empirical and anecdotal evidence against it, humans have been conditioned to believe that we can beat the market. It's not our fault. While I think that the media can sometimes be at fault for creating misperceptions, the truth of the matter is that human nature bears most of the blame for these erroneous and sometimes dangerous beliefs. We're emotional creatures. We sense things. We have gut feelings. We have imaginations. Our brains are finely honed so as to survive the most brutal, uncertain conditions in the wild. These biases influence our behavior, which has historically had a negative impact on our investment decisions. The study of this phenomenon is called behavioral finance.

One of the foremost leaders in the study of behavioral finance is Meir Statman, a professor of finance at Santa Clara University. His research into the causes of irrational investing by otherwise rational people is both fascinating and exceptionally insightful. Statman has identified three common biases and has developed a framework that Gen Y can use to overcome the mistakes that past generations have made (and, in some cases, continue to make). By understanding the tendencies of human nature and applying that knowledge, we can make better investment decisions, which may lead to a greater chance of financial success.

Action Bias

Action bias is the need to do something, anything, in the presence of chaos. As the U.S. Marines say, "The worst decision is indecision." It's a fairly important bias to have and one that developed in humans over millennia. Imagine yourself several thousand years ago sitting around a fire with your tribe. Suddenly, arrows whiz by your head, and you hear dogs barking in the distance. Choosing to sit and contemplate will get you killed. Picking up the nearest rock, finding cover, or taking any action may save your life.

It's still an important bias today. One particularly rainy day, my wife and I discovered that our roof was leaking. Water was dripping down from the ceiling in our guest room and had already soaked the bed, pooled on the floor, and was making its way into the rest of the house. Neither of us knew what to do. We have no roofing experience between us. But the other option was sit idly by while the rest of our home and our belongings were impacted by this leak. I did the only thing I could think to do: I ran out and bought a tarp at Home Depot, and we both climbed onto our roof (a first for both of us) and covered the area where we thought the leak was. I'm not sure a roofing expert would have followed these exact steps, but something was better than nothing in this case because we stopped the flow of water and minimized the damage to our home. So action bias seems like a great life lesson to live by, right? Not so when it comes to investment strategy.

Let me take you back to the nightmare of a conference call my firm hosted for our clients in the middle of the great 2008-2009 crash. Clients were scared that the market was going to go to zero. There seemed to be no money, banks were failing left and right, and every client demanded to know the same thing: "What are the next steps you are going to take to stop the bleeding in my portfolio?" This is textbook action bias; my clients wanted action in the presence of chaos.

The problem was that "doing something, anything," would have likely caused more damage to our clients' portfolios at the time. In this case, the correct course of action was something called systematic rebalance. All our investments are made using a model portfolio so that when the market tanks (note: when the market tanks, not if) our clients can maintain composure. The only trades we place are to rebalance to the model. If we choose to be unprincipled and fall victim to emotional responses, we doom ourselves to the same fate as those who try to time the market. Unfortunately, this strategy of systemic rebalance looks a lot like inaction to an outsider. How to explain this to a (rightfully) panicked investor? As humans, we were going against an instinct to do something. In the end, our strategy of "doing something by doing nothing" was not good enough for some of our clients. Several pulled all their money out of the market, and a few just flat-out fired us. Those who stayed and didn't panic recovered over a couple years.

Action bias is much like a nervous flier on a commercial airline. They board the plane, likely knowing that the probability of the flight crashing is close to 0%. The flight takes off, everything is going smoothly, and the flight attendants start to serve drinks. Suddenly, the plane begins to shake and jerk. It's turbulence, which is a normal part of almost every flight. The probability that the plane will crash has not increased, yet our nervous flier is still suffering a near panic attack. They cannot fly the plane or control the turbulence. All they can do is grip the armrests, ride out the bumps, and trust that the airline they chose is reputable and hires capable pilots to help them land safely.

Nervous investors have a similar experience. They find an advisor (or maybe invest on their own), and they take their hard-earned savings and buy a series of stocks, mutual funds, or other reasonable investments and wait. Almost two-thirds of the time the market is on the rise, so chances are the investor sees at least an initial uptick. But at some point during the year, the market hits a turbulent patch. The nervous investor is now starting to panic. The immediate temptation is for the investor to pull the plug and take all their money out of the market.

It's a good thing that nervous fliers do not have the same power as a nervous investor. Moving all of one's money into cash after a short-term loss in the market is akin to jumping out of a plane with a parachute because some turbulence frightened you. Once you hit the ground, you then have to try to walk or swim to your destination with no road map, no professional guidance, and no support system.

Firing an advisor and taking over one's own portfolio is like walking into the cockpit, relieving the captain of his or her duties, and taking over the controls. Between a pilot and a layperson, the layperson is much more likely to crash the plane. Investors take over or jump out of the plane all the time when the market is going down. In the moment, they feel like they are doing something, which is satisfying. Gratification is great in the moment, but the long-term effects can be disastrous.

Hindsight Bias

With hindsight bias, people tend to say that they should have known what was coming. They go back and think that, had they just listened to their gut, they could have avoided disaster or made a lot of money. It's a form of buyer's remorse.

I still deal with this nearly ten years after the Great Recession of 2008–2009. I can't tell you how many clients and prospective clients come through my door and say they knew that the crash of 2008 was coming. They had applied for a mortgage around that time, and it was too easy. They should have followed their gut at the time and went to cash, because it was so obviously unsustainable. Herein lies the problem: It was not obvious at all. There is a reason why the movie The Big Short only featured a handful of professionals. Every other professional didn't think it was all too obvious.

These clients get down on themselves because they think they should have known better, and they vow to never make the same mistake again, or they decide to hire a professional to help. But many times, the professionals fail to deliver. There are commercials and blogs dedicated to touting how well some guru can predict the future, that they did make the correct call in 2008, and that they can help you not make the same mistake again. In the end, they are reading tea leaves as well.

The problem is that tea leaves are never going to spell out the right move to make to anyone, layman or professional. Sure, after an event has occurred, we look back at those same tea leaves and ask ourselves, "Why couldn't I read these better?" However, no matter how hard we try, the next cup will be no more revelatory than all the prior cups. The dangerous part of hindsight bias is that if at any point we listen to our gut and it works out, we then set ourselves up for confirmation bias.

Confirmation Bias

Hindsight bias piggybacks confirmation bias. When investors let confirmation bias take hold, they tend to accept evidence that confirms their beliefs and reject evidence that does not. We have all sat next to "that person" at the hair salon or bar who says something like, "I knew Apple was going to go gangbusters, so I bought in at $125 a share."

I don't condone violence, but this always makes me want to punch that person in the face. The reason is, our own hindsight bias kicks in. We say to ourselves, "I remember when the guy on the radio was talking about how well Apple was doing. I knew I should have bought some shares." This naturally leads to a feeling of shame because we did not have the same experience or same success (which also ties into representativeness, something we'll explore in the next section).

To avoid a punch-fight, unclench those fists, and let's explore what actually happened here. What our friend has very likely done is engaged in confirmation bias. He wants to believe that he is a good stock-picker and that his own knowledge and expertise led him to make a wise investment choice. This is not likely the case. The average DIY investor underperforms the market significantly. For the average investor over the 20-year period ending December 31, 2014, their return was just 5.2% while the S&P performed at 9.9%.

A DIY investor must resolve this cognitive dissidence somehow. The way the investor does this is through selective memory. In my example, the DIY investor strongly recalls the Apple stock that they purchased at $125 but conveniently (though not maliciously) forgets they purchased Qualcomm at $700 per share, that pesky

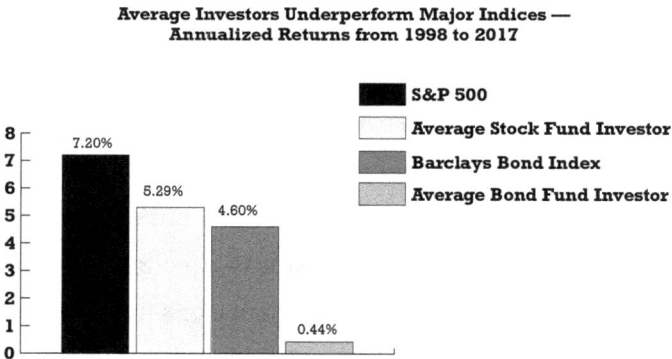

Average stock investor and average bond investor performances [1]

Enron investment, and a myriad of other busts that have recognized significant losses. But this is the nature of the beast.

Take the Great Recession of 2007–2009...and a close relative of mine. I started in the investment industry in 2009, just after the Great Recession. Thankfully, 2009 turned out to be a good year, as did 2010. Sometime in 2010, this relative decided to hire an investment advisor. They did not want me managing their money, and quite honestly, the feeling was mutual.

Nevertheless, I decided to help them find their own advisor and started a conversation.

Me: How are you currently invested?

Relative: 100% cash.

Me: How long have you been in cash?

Relative: Since August 2008, because I knew the market was not sustainable.

Me: How long are you going to be staying in cash?

Relative: As long as the unemployment rate is high.

Me: How high is high?

Relative: I'll know it when I see it.

This relative is not a stupid person, and I think their perspective was probably shared by millions of other Americans.

It was not just my relative or the standard layperson who was shouting "I told you so!" from the rooftops. Many prominent authors and self-proclaimed investment gurus were saying the same thing. Indeed, there is a class of financial experts known as the "Permabears." They continuously believe that the market will tank every year.

One such Permabear is Marc Faber. Mr. Faber has earned the moniker "Dr. Doom" for all his bearish predictions. Certainly, he has some street cred. He predicted the crash of 1987 as well as the crash of 2008. The problem is almost all his predictions since 2000 have been crashes. I'm not sure which adage fits better: Even a blind squirrel occasionally finds a nut, or a broken watch is right two times a day.

Despite the fact he is wrong most of the time, he still has over 12,000 followers on Twitter. There are still people who pay to read his opinions on his website: www.gloomboomdoom.com. Mr. Faber preys on confirmation bias because 44.6% (according to Guru Grades) of the time he gets to say, "I called it." The 12,000 followers on Twitter are able to say the same thing. Whenever the bad event occurs, they all say to each other and, more annoyingly, at cocktail parties, "I felt it in my gut."

Humans all do this to some extent. At least once in our lives, we are the person others want to punch in the face. My wife is always quick to point out that I often end up working into unrelated conversations that I am an attorney, a CPA, and a CFP. What I don't mention to people are all of my failures. I nearly was kicked out of law school. I failed a part of my CPA exam the first time around. I also dedicated eight years of my life to the hammer throw and came up short of All-American my senior year of college. I don't broadcast those bits of information because I don't like to remember them, and I want others to think I am the most successful person they have ever met. (Please stay tuned for upcoming book-signing/face-punching dates.)

Representativeness

Representativeness is assigning a prediction to an event based upon personal experiences with similar events. As a species, this serves us well most of the time. Thousands of years ago, while we were still hunter-gatherers, if we came across a large animal with lots of teeth, we assumed that animal meant us harm. Even if we had never seen such an animal before, we knew, generally, that other dangerous animals we had encountered in our past were large and had lots of teeth.

This logic is still helpful today. While we are outside playing with our kids or sunbathing, we see dark clouds roll in. Experience tells us that dark clouds mean rain. Thus, we go inside to avoid getting wet. But what if it was really an alien race looking to offload all their riches onto the first person they saw? It's a slim possibility—so slim that we risk losing out on interstellar wealth so as not to get soaked.

The problem is that investors have the same mentality. They see the stock market plummet on the news. They immediately recall the dread of opening their statements to see the values of their portfolios decimated in the last crash. Because I live in Silicon Valley, this is especially true. A lot of people in the Bay Area remember the tech crash. They remember their neighbors purchasing second homes and nice cars with the promise of their big payday coming through in the form of stock options or mutual funds specializing in high-tech. Overnight, these paper millionaires disappeared.

When the market goes down, these investors see the worst coming. Worse yet, these ideas were confirmed in 2007–2009 when the market was down 50%. But these signs are not limited to just watching the actual performance of the market, but by ancillary signs as well. People will often look at moving averages, trading volume, and other indicators attempting to assign commonality to prior success stories.

On the face of it, it's a somewhat rational way to go about stock selection. After all, right before Company XYZ stock shot up in price, its 120-day moving average (the average price of a particular stock over a 120-day period) was 20% below the prior year's moving average, the P/E (price to earnings ratio) was above 1.2 for the first time in years, and XYZ's stock had book to market ratio finally above

2.0. And everyone knows that once a stock is classified as growth, it takes off. Thus, since Company ABC stock has the same metrics, it only makes sense that it too should soon see a big price run up. In the end, it's just reading tea leaves.

The problem is that the stock market doesn't work that way. If we keep mathematical probabilities in mind, we must remember that every stock movement is an independent event. Companies have their own board of directors, R&D departments, CEOs, and infrastructure. Their future profits have little to do with their 120-day moving average. That being said, we must be intellectually honest. The truth of the matter is that many people do use the 120-day moving average to predict stock movements.

Hundreds of indicators can be used to predict movements of stock. At any given moment, there is no way to tell which indicator could be the correct one. If the 120-day moving average group trades on a stock but then another group dedicated to the P/E ratio moves on it just out of coincidence, there is a temporary increase in buying of the stock and the price goes up. Both groups of traders get the desired result, and both think that their research has made them money. They have padded their confirmation bias and representativeness bias.

A Hyperactive Kid Goes Passive: My Introduction to Passive Investing

After my Marvel experience I was pretty much done with stocks. My father was in charge of my finances anyway, so giving up control of investing was not a difficult decision. He was smart enough to know that buying individual stocks was not a great idea since he too had been burned by individual stocks and had learned his lesson. He invested in mutual funds, so starting in the mid-1990s he invested in the best funds he could find: Janus and Nicholas

He was not alone. Janus and Nicholas funds were the darlings of the 1990s. They had, after all, a sector specialty: "high-tech." (Does anyone say that anymore?) Everybody loved the new stock market. There was a direct relationship between the financial loss posted in the company's earnings and stock price of the company. The bigger the loss, the seemingly bigger the gain in stock price. But as Che Guevera said in Andrew Lloyd Weber's Evita, "When the money keeps rolling in, you don't ask questions."

Thankfully, I was busy with high school and college and had absolutely no idea that the floor had dropped from my portfolio. I am fairly certain I would have had a heart attack. It was also fortuitous that I did not need the money from the portfolio to pay for college. The same could not be said for some of my classmates. I recall a friend's father playing an important role in one of the first online grocery stores.

During the spring of 2001, I overheard a conversation between my classmate and his parents about which online company was going to go bust next. My parents' work and livelihoods were never dependent upon high-tech, or really any cyclical market, so I'd never paid any attention up to that point. But hearing the fear and uncertainty in my classmate's voice made me realize that the stock market was a bigger deal than just a monthly statement (which I didn't read anyway).

It was at that point I realized that the stock market was a more dangerous place than I'd learned about with my Marvel stock. As I entered law school, I continued to turn a willfully ignorant eye to my investments (which were still in Janus, Nicholas, and Wrigley). I accepted that I was powerless and wisely did what everybody does in default: nothing. I just packed on student debt, took my exams, and tried my hand at internships.

But a funny thing happened on my way to a legal career. First, I met my wife on Jdate.com. (It really works!) Second, I met her father. Many people outside the San Jose community don't know the name Alan Werba, but they should. A pioneer in the financial services industry, he created one of the first companies that brought passive modern portfolio theory-based solutions to the masses.

He wrote a book with his business partners in 1996 called The Prudent Investor's Guide to Beating the Market. The second time I met him he lent me a copy. As soon as I began reading it, I couldn't put it down. For a day and a half I read that book, only stopping to eat and go to the bathroom. (Okay. Fine, I still read it in the bathroom.) I was completely rapt and felt like I was experiencing an awakening. I'm pretty sure I reached a state of nirvana not yet attained by the Dalai Lama himself. My attachment, aversion, and ignorance of the market were extinguished. I was at a place of complete peace.

Does this make me a weirdo? Probably. But its truths set me free. Following are the most important pieces that I discovered:

1. Active management has never consistently worked. (See the section "Active Management: The Best Keno Game in Town" for more on this point.)

2. Control what you can and forget the rest. (See the section "Is the Market Out of Control? Forget About It!" for more on this point.)

We're going to explore these points further below.

Active Management: The Best Keno Game in Town

Keno is a game that is essentially like the lottery. There are a bunch of numbers on a card, and the player picks the numbers he thinks the casino will pick. A formerly wholesome, likeable comedian, Bill Cosby, had a different way to explain it. He used to do a bit where he would ask the audience whether anybody wanted to learn to play the casino game "Keno." Inevitably, someone from the audience would volunteer to go up.

He would then ask the person to take out $20 and hand it over. The person on stage would always comply. Cosby then took the money, put it in his pocket, and said to the audience member, "You lose. That's how you play Keno." The audience would then roar with laughter.

Okay, so active management is not quite the comedian's version of Keno, but it isn't wholly dissimilar either. Active management is a system whereby a fund manager chooses stocks, sectors of stock, or other groupings that they believe will outperform the overall market or some benchmark, and when research says to trade, the manager trades. This yields high amounts of turnover in an actively managed portfolio. It is distinct from passive management when stocks are traded more infrequently. (This is often called a buy-and-hold strategy.) Active managers could be picking new stocks every day. The one certain thing is they believe that they have the research or know-how to do better than everybody else. Remember what we learned a few sections back? Anyone who claims to know the secrets of the market is lying.

The financial industry thrives on active management, and before the 1990s there was really no other game in town for individual investors. The common belief is that investors expected a return higher than the market average, and if you weren't aiming above market average, the only thing you were aiming at was being fired by your clients. Even today, with all the opportunities for passive investing, almost 64% of individual investors go with active management.

Marketwide Active vs. Passive Funds by Dollar Amount

Total assets per trillion of dollars

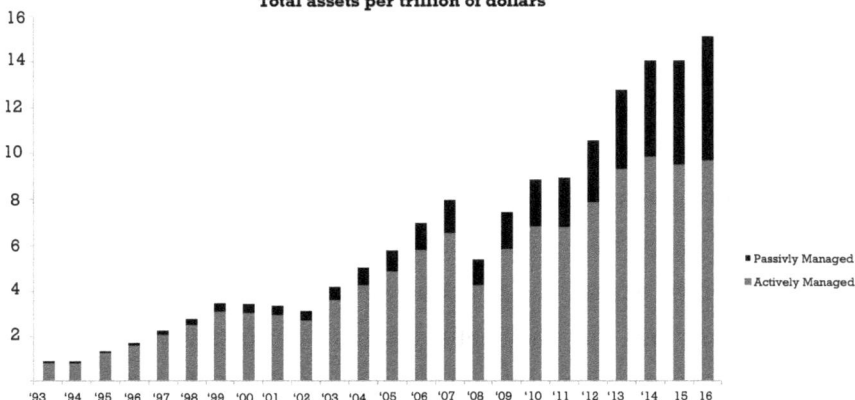

(Source: Loring Ward, Morningstar)

I can't figure out why that is precisely—it could be the romanticism of it all. It's the manager versus the world, acting as the champion for the lowly investor. It can also be a strain of action bias where the investor feels like the manager should be doing something, anything, to maximize returns. It may also be that the average investor likes to think of their advisor as earning their keep.

The one thing I am certain about is that active management does not consistently work, despite the investment industry's claims that there is some expert out there who can pick better than any other expert or algorithm. These claims by the financial industry can be easily disproven and should be summarily dismissed.

The Traditional Choice: Active or Passive

SPIVA U.S. Scorecard 2016
% of Actively Managed Funds which Outperformed the Benchmark

Large CAP Funds vs
S&P 500

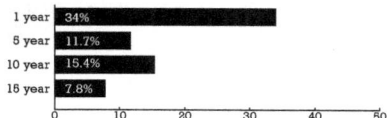

1 year	34%
5 year	11.7%
10 year	15.4%
15 year	7.8%

Small CAP Funds vs
S&P 600

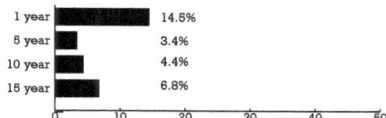

1 year	14.5%
5 year	3.4%
10 year	4.4%
15 year	6.8%

International Funds vs
S&P 700

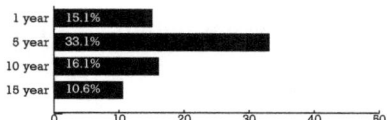

1 year	15.1%
5 year	33.1%
10 year	16.1%
15 year	10.6%

Gorvernment Intermediate vs
Barclays Intermediate Government

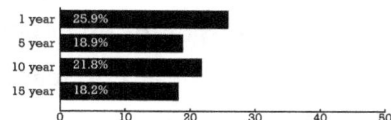

1 year	25.9%
5 year	18.9%
10 year	21.8%
15 year	18.2%

Papa Needs a New Pair of Shoes: Minding the Statistical Mean at the Casino and in Investing

Let me admit something up front. I love Las Vegas. I love everything about the Strip—from the hot sidewalks to the air-conditioned, windowless, is-it-day-or-is-it-night casino floor. I really enjoy gambling, even though you'll never find me at anything more than a $10 minimum table. My favorite game in the entire casino, and the only game I ever play, is craps.

Craps is a dice game played around an oval table. Any player can gather around the table and bet money on what number they think will turn up with the roll of the dice. The shooter (person throwing the dice) wins or loses for the whole table. At its most simple, there is an opening roll where the shooter and table win if there is a seven or eleven, and lose if the dice show two, three, or twelve. Any other number becomes the point. Once the point is set, the shooter must roll the point a second time before rolling a seven to win.

Is this a losing proposition? Absolutely. But is it also super fun, especially when the nice cocktail waitresses bring you free vodka sodas endlessly into a long night that turns into day? Absolutely again. Regardless of my other poor choices in Vegas, when I walk in the casino, I have a very clear vision for my gambling strategy: I know that if I consistently bet the same methodology for an extended period of time, I will return to the statistically driven result. The opposite side of the coin is that the casino knows the same thing. So long as the odds are stacked in the casino's favor, every player who goes for long stretches will leave the casino a little bit lighter in the pocketbook than when they came in.

On one particular visit to Vegas, I happened to walk through the Bellagio in the late evening. I stopped by a craps table where a large crowd had gathered. The table had a minimum bet of $25, so my wallet was firmly in my pocket. I watched as a man about my age put $1,000 on "hard eight" (betting that the next roll of the dice would show two "fours"). The statistical likelihood of this happening is one in 36 rolls. If the number seven (one out of every six rolls) shows before hard eight, the bettor loses. Unbelievably, the next roll was a hard eight, and the guy won $9,000 just like that. But did he quit while he was ahead? Not a chance. This idiot plunked down another $1,000 on hard eight. What did the Fates do? He won again. He was up $18,000 in a matter of minutes.

Was the casino worried? No. They were ecstatic. They now had a guy with very strong confirmation bias who felt invincible. Not only that, nobody surrounding that table was going to leave. Everybody felt great because they now felt like they could win. The bettor was going to be at that table all night, and at some point he'd give every penny of that $18,000 back, and more.

I'm telling you this story because everybody returns to the statistical mean, also called the average. The mean is the mean because it's the mean. Everything returns to the average at some point. There is an exceptionally slim possibility that an outlier occurs. The big winner in the Bellagio had true odds of 36:1, but the casino only pays 9:1. This is the house edge. While the bettor defied the odds and was an outlier in the short term, in the long term he will return to the to the 36:1 odds and he will return all of his winnings at some point if he plays long enough. There will be a time where he plays eight the hard way 50 times in a row and he gets nothing.

Active investing is no different. There are thousands of active funds available. Each one is run by really smart people who received their MBAs from Ivy League universities. They have algorithms that run millions of calculations every second making decisions to buy or sell faster than any human could ever hope. They jockey for position and

High Costs Make Outperformance Difficult

Winners and losers based on expense ratios (%)—equity funds

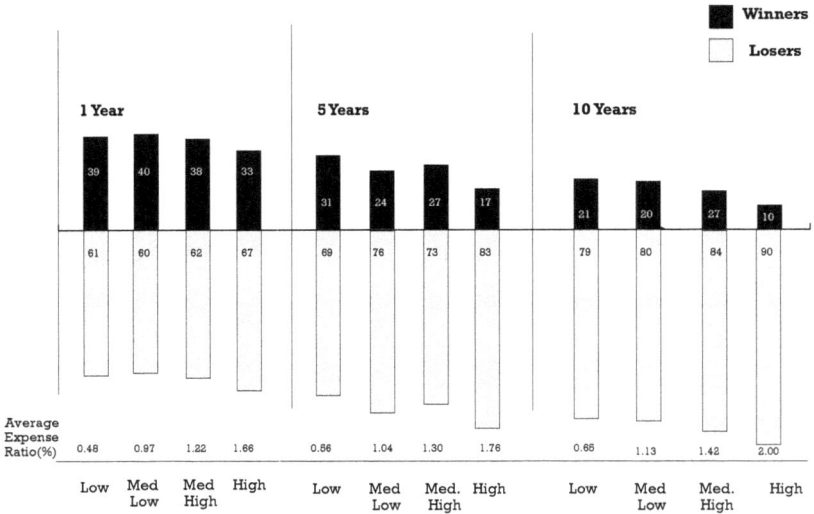

| | Winners |
| | Losers |

	1 Year				5 Years				10 Years			
Winners	39	40	38	33	31	24	27	17	21	20	27	10
Losers	61	60	62	67	69	76	73	83	79	80	84	90
Average Expense Ratio(%)	0.48	0.97	1.22	1.66	0.86	1.04	1.30	1.76	0.65	1.13	1.42	2.00
	Low	Med Low	Med High	High	Low	Med Low	Med High	High	Low	Med Low	Med High	High

try to outduel one another on a minute-to-minute, day-by-day, and year-by-year basis.

Taking cost out of the equation, there almost certainly will be a normal distribution curve where a tiny percentage will greatly outperform others, a small percentage will somewhat outperform, a majority will be average, a small percentage will underperform, and a tiny percentage will greatly underperform.

Cost is worth some discussion, though. Nothing drags a portfolio down quite like cost. The average actively traded mutual fund's internal cost (commonly known as a fund's "expense ratio") is around 1.5%, which means that before the investor makes any money, the fund manager gets paid their 1.5%.

Poor Track Record for Active Managers

Percentage of Active Funds that Outperformed Their Index 2008 - 2017

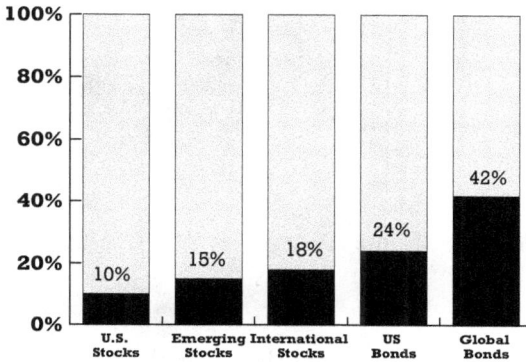

Even if the mutual fund returns 0%, the investor will experience a loss of at least 1.5%. What's more, actively traded mutual funds tend to have higher turnover ratios. Experts estimate that a 100% turnover ratio costs somewhere between 0.36% and 1% in addition to the internal cost. This means on average an investor who uses an actively managed fund may have a 1.86% to 2.5% hurdle to overcome each year. The investor makes nothing until the fund makes 1.86% to 2.5%.

When adjusted for internal cost, a comparison of active funds to benchmarks isn't even close. Active funds are not able to keep pace. From January 2007 to December 2016, almost 83% of U.S.-focused active managers failed to beat their index (S&P 1500), as did 84% of International Large Cap (S&P 700) active managers (Standard & Poor's 2016). From 2007 through 2016, there was no sector of the

Do Those 'Winning' Managers Persist?

Number of Funds that stay in Top Quartile

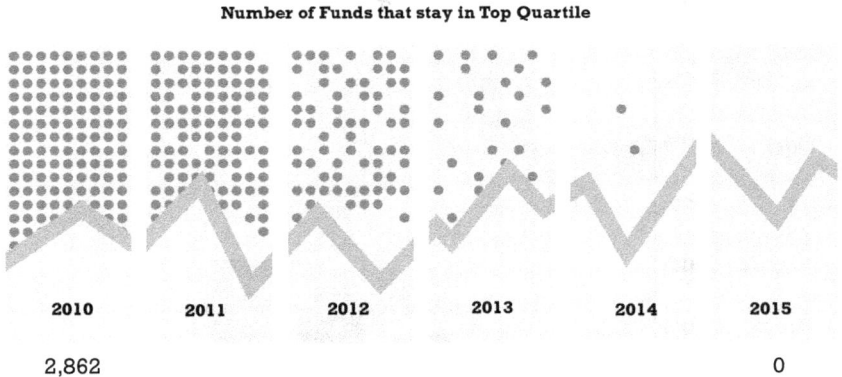

2010	2011	2012	2013	2014	2015
2,862					0

market where active managers beat their benchmark more often than not.

An investor who randomly chose an active manager would more likely than not (and sometimes by a lot) do worse than the benchmark. Not only that, if the investor paid an investment advisor on top, they would lose another percentage. Choosing to hitch your financial future to active management is just like the casino—the odds are not in your favor. From 2002 through 2012, active managers outperformed index funds by 0.12% before fees. Tack on the fees, and it's not even close.

However, many investors feel like they are the exception, that they can pick the funds or hire someone to pick the funds that will defy statistics. While this is a fool's errand on its face, it does merit some discussion. Not surprising, even if an investor or a professional picks a very competent fund that does well in one year, that does not necessarily mean the same fund will do well the next year.

In fact, when we look to find which managers consistently outperform the market, we lose even more heart than just looking at a single year. Of all the U.S. equity managers in the top quartile in 2010, only 2.1% were still in the top quartile at the end of 2015. I believe that professional advisors fared no better than laymen when it came to selecting the correct funds.

This was the exact mistake that my father made in the mid to late 1990s. He went with the hot hand. He didn't do anything wrong, and he certainly wasn't alone in choosing to ride tech stocks. The media was inundating the whole country with the "New Economy" and how everybody should get on board with high-tech.

Statistics caught up to Janus and Nicholas. Stock and sector-pickers are subject to the law of averages. They cannot continue at a breakneck pace forever. When you pick stocks or sectors, you almost by definition have to end up coming back down to earth, and you end up shooting yourself in the foot most of the time anyway.

Is the Market Out of Control? Forget About It!

I was once in a Bible study. Every week for a year I studied a different section of the five books of Moses until I had read them all. After reading each section, the group would go to the leader's house and talk about the section. During one of the sections we were reading, the topic of death came up. As we discussed mourning rituals, the leader noted there was a cap on how long the Bible tells us to mourn: twelve months for a parent and one month for a spouse, sibling, or child. The leader reasoned this is for the protection of the mourner not to dwell too long on the death of a loved one. He then said something truly profound: "One of the greatest gifts God has given us is the ability to forget."

Losing money in your portfolio is in no way akin to losing a loved one; however, it does sting. I know people who check their portfolios every day. When the market goes up, we are reminded of the gains, and when the market goes down, we are constantly reminded that we are getting poorer (even though temporarily). There is actually another bias that isn't financial in nature that hinders us as investors: loss aversion. As humans, we would rather not suffer loss than experience gain.

Every time you check your portfolio, especially in a down market, you activate this bias, and as a result, you are prone to make bad decisions. Remember that terrible conference call with all my firm's clients in late 2008. The market had gone very dark and was about to get darker. As we told clients not to worry and to stay the course, we all knew that everyone wanted to bail. All biases kicked in: action, confirmation, hindsight, and loss aversion. Panic was in the air.

Our greatest enemies at the time were the statements and reporting being sent to clients. Of course, clients always have a right to know what is going on in their accounts, but knowing too much heightens one's awareness of the loss. Our clients felt helpless, and we, as advisors, felt helpless as well because no one really controls the market.

Control is an illusion. No single entity controls the stock market: not the Illuminati, not the Freemasons, and not the Jews. (If they did, I'd be pretty angry since I haven't received my cut.) If you can't control it, why worry about it? Once an investor makes the commitment to put resources into the stock market, hand wringing is not going to help the return. If an investor is constantly in a state of panic about the market, they shouldn't be so heavily invested.

When the market goes down, there is nothing that you can do. Action bias will lead you down the path of ruin. You will be tempted to sell, but that is not going to change the market. The only thing it will do is ruin your chance for a recovery. Hindsight bias will do you no good. You can't turn back the clock. Markets are cyclical. Confirmation bias leads back to action bias, which is a dangerous place to be.

What you can do is control the controllables. You control the risk in your own portfolio, so before investing, take a hard look at the losses you're willing to endure before getting in the market. If you decide during a down market that you want to be less heavily invested, at least wait for the recovery to make a change.

You control the diversification of the portfolio. You don't have to be in a single stock or just a handful. You can choose to use modern portfolio theory (discussed in Chapter 6) to your advantage and diversify away many of the risks endemic to high-concentration positions. You can use the three-factor model (also to be discussed in Chapter 6) to take the risks worth taking.

You can control the cost. Mutual funds can destroy portfolio returns by internal charges that can reach 2% or more. By using low-cost options, such as exchange traded funds (ETF) (discussed in Chapter 6) or passive indices, you can reduce that cost and increase your return both in up markets and in down markets. Actively managed funds mainly increase cost with very little additional return to show for it.

Check, Please!

As you begin your foray into investing, keep the following four points in mind to retain your sanity and get the most long-term bang for your buck:

1. **Your brain is not your friend.** Your brain is wired to survive on the savannahs of Africa and avoid being eaten by a bigger animal. Investing is not something your brain is evolved to do.

2. **The passive versus active debate is well settled.** Active investing typically does worse than passive. Passive is lower cost, can be more diversified, and is strategic in nature. Choosing active investing is a notch better than playing Keno...maybe.

3. **It's great to be average.** With all of the investment world trying to outdo itself and win an impossible game, you can opt

out. By riding the market instead of trying to outsmart it, you can be at peace with your investments. More importantly, you can also beat the experts.

Control what you can and forget the rest. There are a lot of things to worry about in life, but the stock market is not one of them. Nothing any individual can do can control the way the market moves, and no amount of worrying can increase your return. Focus on what you can control: diversification, cost, and getting into the right risk level for you.

Endnote

1 *Average stock investor and average bond investor performances were used from a DALBAR study, Quantitative Analysis of Investor Behavior (QAIB), 03/2018. QAIB calculates investor returns as the change in assets after excluding sales, redemptions, and exchanges. This method of calculation captures realized and unrealized capital gains, dividends, interest, trading costs, sales charges, fees, expenses, and any other costs. After calculating investor returns in dollar terms (above), two percentages are calculated: Total investor return rate for the period and annualized investor return rate. Total return rate is determined by calculating the investor return dollars as a percentage of the net of the sales, redemptions, and exchanges for the period. The fact that buy-and-hold has been a successful strategy in the past does not guarantee that it will continue to be successful in the future. Equities, bonds, and other asset classes have different risk profiles, which should be considered when investing. Bonds are subject to market and interest rate risk. Bond values will decline as interest rates rise and/or issuer's creditworthiness declines, and are subject to availability and changes in price. Stock investing involves risks, including increased volatility (up and down movement in the value of your assets) and loss of principal. The S&P 500 is an index of 500 stocks chosen for market size, liquidity and industry grouping, among other factors. The S&P 500 is designed to be a leading indicator of U.S. equities and is meant to reflect the risk/return characteristics of the large cap universe. The Bloomberg Barclays US Aggregate Bond Index ("Barclays Bond Index") covers the USD-denominated, investment-grade, fixed-rate, taxable bond market of SEC-registered securities. The index includes bonds from the Treasury, Government-Related, Corporate, MBS (agency fixed-rate and hybrid ARM passthroughs), ABS, and CMBS sectors. Indexes are unmanaged baskets of securities that investors cannot directly invest in. Index returns do not take into consideration any fees.*

CHAPTER 4

College: Priceless Memories for About $500,000 a Pop

People ask me all the time how to make sure that they have enough wealth to last them through retirement. My answer is always the same: "Don't get married, and don't have kids." That is an extreme statement, and I'm only (half) kidding, of course, but if we're strictly talking about the fastest path to retirement...this is it. Children are enormously expensive. The average cost of raising a child in the U.S. is $245,000, and when you get to the coasts, it gets closer to $500,000.

If you think that number is hard to swallow, the time value of money really twists the knife. If, instead of spending $28,000 per year for a child, you placed that money into an account that earned 7% per year for 18 years and then you stashed it away for another 20 years until retirement, you would end up with almost $3.7 million. By that calculation, my three children are going to end up costing me around $11 million. And that's before college.

I promise you, I love my kids, but as a financial planner, I am compelled (and paid!) to study the economics of child-rearing. In this chapter, we are going to take a hard look at the costs associated with having kids. We'll then dive deeper into the abyss of planning for college, including exploring options that do not involve the typical 529 Plan. Finally, we'll discuss how to start teaching children about money so that they won't make the same mistakes their predecessors made.

Children Are Life's Greatest ~~Joy~~ Expense

As mentioned, my wife and I have three children. We love them dearly, and they are always perfect little angels who never fight, yell, or destroy the house. My wife and I were totally prepared for the responsibility and cost of being parents, and I'm definitely not writing this crouched in a cramped den, hiding from the chaos and nursing my latest Lego-related foot injury.

Now that you've read a bit of my next fantasy novel, let's get a few things straight about having kids. First, as much as you will hear me complain about my three beautiful daughters, they are the best thing that has ever happened to me. It's like knowing what ice cream is and thinking you could be happy just eating that for the rest of

your life, then discovering hot fudge, sprinkles, whipped cream...
you get the idea. Finally, and most importantly, as we've already
established, children are expensive. So if you plan to have children,
you need to plan for what it's going to cost if you want to have a
comfortable life and retirement.

Whoever you are, you can probably guess what some of the "big
ticket" items are for welcoming a new baby: car seats ($300 every
couple of years), a stroller ($400 for a nice but not over-the-top
version), diapers (incalculable), a crib (starting at $200; $800 for a
nice one), clothing (never ending), and formula. (Who's keeping
track? The kid has to eat.)

Consider these things the tip of the iceberg. Like the iceberg, 90%
of the cost of raising a child lurks "below the surface." Stuff just adds
up. Your child will throw up more than a frat boy during rush week.
They don't just throw up on their stuff; they throw up on your stuff
too. You may be thinking, "Don't they have spit-up blankets?" Yes,
they do, but your baby will only throw up when you don't have one.

You'll be told to swaddle your baby, which is basically wrapping
them up like a burrito. The swaddle blankets will cost $40 a pack.
Why so much? Because they can charge that much. Crib sheet sets
can weigh down your budget. You'll need more than one set because
...babies. Of course, you'll likely want the set that matches the theme
of your baby's room, which is, of course, only available at Pottery
Barn Kids for the low, low price of too expensive.

In a couple of short years, your child will be ready for activities. Spending money on activities will be crucial to their development, you'll be told. You'll be a bad parent if you skimp on developmental activities, you'll be told. So you'll start with soccer, which starts at an obnoxiously early age (Mommy & Me soccer at two, four-versus-four soccer at three). Don't forget you'll need a uniform, ball, shoes, shin guards, and league fees. That's just for one season. And it doesn't end at just soccer. There are equivalent fees and gear required for karate, swim, dance, piano, and parkour. (It exists; Google: "Daniel Tosh Parkour".)

Then your child goes to school. If you are paying for private school, that's when the pain really starts. In Silicon Valley a good private school will cost $15,000 to $20,000 per year. The top-tier schools are closer to $40,000. That's not tax deductible, by the way. And if you send your kids to public school, you've likely paid more for a home in a good district, so you end up getting it from both ends on the education front.

When it comes to birthdays and other gift-giving occasions, the expenses just increase. Gifts are easy when kids are small. What gift do you give a baby? A book, adorable outfit, or other inexpensive toy. What gift do you give a twelve-year-old? That's when you find yourself standing in line at 4:00 a.m. on Black Friday so you can beat the crowds and get the latest video game console before it sells out. Yay, parenting!

All this is not meant to scare you...it's meant to TERRIFY you. Not enough people think about children in terms of dollars and cents. I know there is no possible way to quantify the existence of a human being that you bring into this world, but I wouldn't be doing my job if I didn't educate you on how to calculate the cost of raising kids while still protecting your own retirement and standard of living. (You're someone's baby too!) It's not impossible to raise children and also save/invest responsibly, but it all starts with awareness.

Prepare for Sticker Shock—The Rising Cost of College

Get ready for this: By the year 2030, Yale will cost $150,000 per year if the current trajectory of college tuition maintains course. According to FinancialAid.org, college costs are increasing 5% to 8% per year. Today, the cost of attending Yale University's undergraduate program is about $65,725.

So what is Yale worth? The market says that, very soon, it will be worth a mansion in most parts of the United States.

So maybe Yale is a lofty benchmark for what college will cost for your children. The point is, an already expensive, arguably crucial part of your child's development is going to become borderline unaffordable if you don't start planning now.

For the parents out there who plan to cover every red cent of their child's "Yale-sized" education, you will need about $600,000 sitting in an account by the time your child graduates high school. As a back-of-the-envelope calculation, if you were getting a tax-free rate of return of 7.2%, you would need to start with a $170,000 investment when your child is born, or be able to set aside $1,363 per month every month until your child turns 18.

If this sounds like a lot of money to you, you're not alone. There aren't many young couples who can do that kind of saving between house, kids, and retirement. Even with grandparents helping, for most Americans it's just not possible to save that much for one child, let alone two. Saving for a premier college is like drinking a lake—it's probably not going to happen, and it's incredibly discouraging. Does this mean that we give up? Never! We are millennials. There's a life hack for this.

First, remember that we are using a worst-case scenario tuition amount for this calculation. Based on admission statistics alone, your Baby Einstein will likely not be accepted into Yale or another Ivy League with comparable tuition, so celebrate your average child! Your snowflake can still receive a fantastic education at a great school with lower tuition, which makes a savings target more realistic.

Second, the world is going through a shift in the way it thinks about college. When I was an undergrad, the way you went to class was to have your butt in a seat. If you wanted to do additional coursework over the summer while you were at home, you had to find a college near your house that offered summer classes and you put your butt in that seat. But even a few short years later, this way of thinking has changed.

In 2006, when my wife was one class away from completing her graduate degree in public health from Xavier University in Chicago, we had to move to California so that I could study and take the bar exam. We thought we were going to have to find a seat for her butt in California so that she could finish those last units. Instead, she took a less expensive online course from Mountain State University in West Virginia—and graduated with flying colors, I might add.

More recently, I was thinking about getting a Masters in Law (LLM) in Tax, and I discovered that NYU had an online program. I would have to spend a couple of weeks per year in New York (butt in seat, of course), but, otherwise, the program could be completed entirely over the Web. It's not a perfect system yet, though. The tuition would have been the same; the only cost savings was that I would not have to live in pricey New York City. This was, of course, disappointing since the marginal cost to NYU of me attending their online classes was almost nil. I understand why they do this. If online students received a significant price break, then almost nobody would choose to do classes in person. This will not be the case forever. At some point, there will be a cheaper system.

In addition to less expensive and more widespread online education options, students are going to be able to take some responsibility themselves for paying for college. Arizona State University has partnered up with Starbucks to offer all their baristas an option to receive a four-year degree online while they work. Starbucks will generously cover all of the tuition costs for their employees, and it's a great deal for ASU because the additional cost for more online students is almost nothing. This is just one example, but others are sure to follow.

In sum, parents should not despair. There is real innovation coming out of universities, and I suspect that in the next few years we'll see many new programs that give students the flexibility to take more ownership of their own education, which is a real return to where we were thirty or more years ago.

All of this being said, parents still should be saving for at least part of their children's education. There are a number of tools available that help ease the burden of sending a child to college, but understanding how they should be leveraged is key in making good decisions on where to put long-term, higher education-dedicated dollars.

529 Plans—College or Die

When most people think of saving for college in special accounts, the 529 Plan is the first thing that comes to mind. 529 Plans are also called Qualified Tuition Programs (QTPs). There is a reason why the 529 Plan is considered the gold standard in saving for college: It represents the ability to put after-tax money into an account that grows tax-free so long as the beneficiary uses the proceeds for qualified tuition expenses. All the earnings and capital gains are tax-free, which, if started early, can add up. States get to set the caps on their 529 Plans. These caps range from $235,000 to more than $400,000. Once the beneficiary has reached these numbers, no additional contributions are allowed in that plan, although it can still grow with the market.

However, 529 Plans do come with a catch: If the cash in the account is unused by the beneficiary, a new beneficiary must be selected (see below) who spends the money for educational purposes only. If the money is spent for non-educational purposes, then the gains in the account are taxed at the taxpayer's marginal rate (not capital gains), and there is a 10% penalty on the earnings portion of the distribution. Before starting a 529 Plan, you'll want to be very certain that the cash saved will be used for college education.

To start a 529 Plan, all you need is the following:

1. An owner

2. A beneficiary

3. An approved plan

The owner should be anyone you deem responsible enough to make decisions about pulling the money out of the account, making distributions, and changing beneficiaries (subject to some limitations). Owners are typically the parents. However, if you don't trust the parents of the child, you can substitute in other parents, grandparents, godparents, aunts/uncles, etc.

The beneficiary is the person who is meant to receive the funds in the 529 Plan. For the purposes of this section, we have been discussing the beneficiary as being your child, but it can actually be anyone for whom you want to cover college tuition. I know my kids could always use another 529 Plan, you generous soul, you.

Keep in mind, this beneficiary can change. If you select your child as beneficiary and they decide for whatever reason not to attend college, you (or whomever you've selected as the owner) can decide to change the beneficiary. However, the owner is restricted to a specific list of people who can replace the original beneficiary. The new beneficiary must be related to the original beneficiary in one of the following ways:

1. Son, daughter, stepchild, foster child, adopted child, or a descendant of any of them

2. Brother, sister, stepbrother, or stepsister

3. Father or mother or ancestor of either

4. Stepfather or stepmother

5. Son or daughter of a brother or sister

6. Brother or sister of father or mother

7. Son-in-law, daughter-in-law, father-in-law, mother-in-law, brother-in-law, or sister-in-law

8. The spouse of any individual listed above

9. First cousin

Finally, the plan. Plans are run by the state in which you live. The mechanics are somewhat simple, but there is some nuance. There are generally two types of 529 Plans:

Prepaid Tuition Plan

Because all 529 Plans are run by individual states, those states typically have plans that let the donor pre-pay tuition for the beneficiary at a state school, but not every state school, so read the 529 Plan details carefully. This means that even if tuition increases, the beneficiary will not have to pay anything additional.

Of course, many students do not end up going to a state school in their home state, which means that the prepaid tuition could end up being for nothing. This doesn't mean that you have to forfeit your dollars, but it does mean that you are going to have to accept whatever rate of return the state has credited you with. They may give you the rate at which the in-state tuition has risen (which may not be that great for a state school).

College Savings Plan

This is the more common type of plan, although it doesn't come without complications. The variance from state to state is astounding, and all the flavors and tax consequences are what really add to the complexity surrounding 529 Plans. Some states will give their residents tax deductions for using their own state's 529 Plan. Illinois is a great example of this. Each parent can deduct up to $10,000 on their tax return per year, provided they use the state's college savings plan. California has no such deduction. I've checked—several times.

The plans also widely vary by the investment options and rules. The investment options are as varied as the rest of the investment world. They mostly involve mutual funds; some are actively managed, and some are passively managed. The fees inside the plan can vary widely as well. The basic fees are a program manager fee, a state fee, and a maintenance fee. While the necessity of the fees is debatable, what is not debatable is their impact on return. Fees matter! They eat into your returns, and unless you are getting some serious bang for your buck, you want to keep these fees as low as possible.

Some plans have expense ratios (discussed in Chapter 3) as high as 2.4%. This includes both internal expense ratios and those outside the mutual fund. Nevertheless, a 2.4% hurdle is very difficult to overcome. There are also plans that require the investor to have an advisor. Advisor accounts can be expensive, depending on the sales charge. Some sales charges can be front loaded, which means the investor loses a certain percent (sometimes as high as 5%) upon initial investment and when any money is added to the account.

Not Sure College Is Right for Your Infant? Try ESAs.

My mother tells me that when I was very little she wasn't all that sure that I was going to be college bound, and until I went to law school she kept cash in the house to bail me out of jail. It was hard for my parents to imagine that I, a young lad with a short attention span and copious amounts of energy, would have the discipline and focus to make it through all the required college prep, let alone the upper levels of academia. (Ha! Look at me now, Ma!) There may be some parents out there who feel the same way. First, let me serve as proof that even a crazy four-year-old who couldn't sit for longer than 15 seconds will grow up...somewhat. Second, if you really want to hedge your college bets but still want to save some money tax-free, try an Education Savings Account (ESA), previously called a Coverdell Account.

The basics of an ESA are similar to that of a 529 Plan. Typically, there is an owner with a designated beneficiary. There are adjusted gross income (AGI) caps that apply to the donor. Once a single person's income exceeds $110,000 and a married couple's $220,000, they may no longer make contributions, and the total amount that can be contributed for any one beneficiary across all donors is $2,000 per year. Additionally, contributions cannot be made for a beneficiary once they turn 18.

Account balances must be distributed by the time a beneficiary reaches age 30. At that point, the balance can be moved to the same qualified relatives as listed in 529 Plans, or the beneficiary can bite the bullet and pay the tax. Like the 529 Plan, there are penalties on the earnings should the beneficiary use the money for anything other than education. Also like the 529 Plan, the ESA can be used to save for education with after-tax dollars, and so long as the proceeds are used for education, there is no tax on the earnings or penalties for withdrawal.

However, the ESA has a couple of advantages over the 529 Plan. First, "education" is defined as any education, including college, but also including primary and secondary school. If Grandma and Grandpa want to put some money aside when the child is born, that money can be used for early private education.

Second, the states don't run ESA plans. That means that there is more leeway as to how the money is invested to make it grow. It can hold stocks, bonds, mutual funds, or ETFs of the controlling person's choosing. Individuals can work with their own advisors to get their preferred investment solutions. Costs can be controlled more easily with ESAs since there isn't necessarily an administrative expense, though custodians may charge more.

Timmy Still Chewing on Rocks? Try Custodial Accounts.

Even though my parents didn't have confidence that education was my thing, they still wanted to save for me, just in case. So they started a custodial account for me. The custodial account has several features that distinguish it from other education-type savings mechanisms. The first and most important feature of the custodial account is that the funds need not be used for education, and there are far fewer restrictions.

In a custodial account, the child is the technical owner of the account. Their name and Social Security number are on the tax records that get reported to the IRS. The guardian, typically also the custodian, is supposed to act in the child's best interest. Because the account legally belongs to the child, the guardian cannot use those assets to pay for things that they themselves are otherwise legally obligated to pay for (like food, shelter, etc.). The funds can be used for education, or to help purchase a house or car for the child. However, once the child turns 18 (or 21 in some states), they get unfettered access to the money.

Taxes can sometimes get more complicated with a custodial account. Dividends and interest are taxed at ordinary rates, except where dividends are considered qualified. When securities are sold, there are either capital gains or a loss associated with that sale. All of the income is placed onto the child's tax return. However, just because the income ends up on a child's tax return doesn't mean it gets taxed at the child's rate (See Chapter 2).

While flexibility is a major positive for custodial accounts, many people don't like them because it cedes too much control to the child who may not be ready for any significant sum of money in their late teens/early twenties. Custodial accounts are also taxed in the current year and can be complicated, depending on the amount of income that is earned.

Making Sure Your Family Is Taken Care Of If You Aren't There To Do It

As you marry or reach other "adulting" milestones, it is typically a good time to start thinking about an estate plan. You don't necessarily have to establish one right away when you have no dependents, but once you decide to have children, the game changes entirely.

When a child is born, it's imperative that parents create an estate plan, and fast. Any parent who doesn't have at least a will in place is acting irresponsibly, especially in a state like California where holographic (handwritten) wills are perfectly legal. There's simply no excuse for not making a sound plan for your child should you die unexpectedly.

A basic estate plan (See Chapter 10) should always include a few things:

» **Trust**: The primary function of the trust is to dictate where your assets (house, car, etc.) go upon your passing and keep your estate out of the court system.
» **Will(s):** If you are married, then each of you will sign a will, the purpose of which is to catch assets that were not put in the trust and to inform the Court of your wishes for where minor children

should be placed.

» **Power of attorney:** Assigns decision-making responsibility to someone else in case of your incapacitation.

» **Health care power of attorney:** Authorizes someone else to make medical decisions on your behalf.

The estate plan-making process is not free. A run-of-the-mill estate plan is going to cost at least $2,000 from an attorney that specializes in estate planning, but it's worth every penny. In absence of an estate plan, you defer to your state's best judgement. There is a probate code that says where your assets go, and a person in a robe with a gavel tells your children what's in their best interest and where they get to live. If you think you know better than a stranger about what to do with your kids, make an estate plan.

Teaching Gen Z the Ropes of Personal Finance

No one can humble a grown-up the way a child can. As part of my job, I give talks to parents on how to teach their children about money. I have a whole lecture outlining an entire system of teaching savings, giving, and responsibility to children; when to start giving children money (around age four); and how to set expectations and boundaries. At these events, I can't wait for the Q&A at the end where I get to show off all my money wisdom for the masses. I am your money guy...and I can do anything!

Then I had children of my own. And I actually tried to put into practice what I preach. Turns out, I'm a complete fool and don't know anything (which my wife and mother could have told you). The week after my eldest daughter turned four, my wife and I sat her down and had a heart to heart with her about money. We told her about her allowance, and we explained that if she wanted more money to buy her favorite toys or go to the movies, she was going to have to earn it by taking on tasks around the house.

The first few weeks went fine. Like clockwork, every Sunday, she did some work around the house and earned her weekly allowance. I thought to myself, "Wow! I am even more impressive than I had originally imagined." Then one day, inexplicably, she just lost interest in the whole concept of allowance. Her weekly chores were forgotten about, and the responses were at best nonchalant when I would remind her about all the money she was leaving on the table. This was not going to fly. I'm the money guy! My daughter must learn about money! I resorted to threats. "Honey, if we go to Target and you see a toy you want, I'm not going to buy it for you." She didn't care. I tried again at five, but again, no interest. My dreams of having a mini-Money Honey were completely dashed.

This is all to say that while I have a lot of sage wisdom to impart upon all parents, teaching children about money is not a science... it's more like potty-training. While we may want to force the issue because it is so important, children are just going to be ready when they are ready. The earlier kids learn about money management, the better, but when both parent and child are overly frustrated, take a break. Like the Chicago Cubs of old, I'll try again next year.

GISS This

Nancy Phillips is a children's author who writes a series called the "Zela Wela Kids." She also wrote a booklet called "The Parent's Guide to Kids and Money." In this booklet, Phillips explores a concept called GISS, which stands for Give, Invest, Save, and Spend. While her model for cash management is too simplistic for adults to live by because it does not include debt or taxes, it's a great guideline for kids to follow as they start to learn about money.

The general rules that Phillips lays out are that 10% of one's income should go to charity, 15% should be allocated to investment, 25% should be put in savings, and the balance 50%, should be used for current spending.

Before adding on layers of complexity, let's see how a child would use the model for their allowance. Let's assume that we have a 10-year-old child. Based upon Phillips' recommendations, children should be given a dollar a week for every year of their age, so our 10-year-old would be receiving $10 a week.

Using GISS, $1 a week would go to charity, $1.50 would be invested, $2.50 would go into savings, and $5 could be used for discretionary weekly spending.

In my experience preparing tax returns, very rarely did I see a client give 10% of their income, net or gross, to charity. I won't start a debate here about how much is appropriate to give annually, but I do believe it is important as children develop to teach them empathy and about how to appreciate what they have and help the less fortunate. So based on that, how does our youngster decide where his $52 of annual charitable giving should go? Encourage your children to think big about who they want to help with their money. Do they want to help kids in their local community? Across the world? Animals? The environment? As your child grows, their ideals may change, but I can't think of a better way to get our kids involved in thinking locally and globally and of people other than themselves.

The next bucket that he or she will put money into is the investment portion. Contributing $1.50 a week may not seem like a lot, but don't be fooled; this is arguably the most important bucket for our 10-year-old. Albert Einstein apocryphally called compound interest the eighth wonder of the world and named it the most powerful force in the universe. For the man who understood gamma rays and relativity, this was no small statement. If a child were to invest $1.50 a week for 10 years, that child would accumulate $1,067.94, assuming a 6% constant rate of return, which is a reasonable assumption. Although the small weekly investment may not cover college in eight years, the point is to show, in real life, what the power of compound interest can do. Emphasize that this money will be used for things like college, starting a business, or other income-producing concepts that are easier to grasp.

There is another lesson to be had in this situation as well. In my assumptions, I have a 6% constant rate of return. As any investor knows, returns are never constant, and 6% may or may not be the right assumption. In this way, our 10-year-old would learn how the stock market works and a little bit about appetite for risk, as we discussed in Chapter 3.

Next would be the decision on savings, and under Phillips' method, our 10-year-old would put $2.50 away for near-term use. This is distinctly different from investment. For savings, there is a specific goal in mind. For a 10-year-old, that may be as big as an Xbox, new bike, or other relatively big-ticket item. The idea is to save money for an item that is too costly to be acquired from weekly cash flow. Because there are going to be so many items that will far exceed this 10-year-old's $5/week spending limit, savings will be a very important category. Writing out a goal and keeping your eyes on the prize are important lessons to learn here. It could very well take our 10-year-old over half of a year to get a game that they really want. It requires prioritization and delayed gratification.

Finally, there is the spending category. Again, kids should use this bucket to buy things that they want now. They will likely make some bad decisions with it, like using it all to buy candy bars, music on iTunes, or some other item that would temporarily delight a 10-year-old. Of course, something to point out here is that unused cash can be added to the other categories and most probably augment savings.

Obviously, a child's desires go much farther than their allowance will take them. Informed parents will find ways to help their kids achieve their goals but also do it in a consultative way to teach kids early lessons about giving, investing, saving, and spending.

Make Them Work for It

Leading up to my law school graduation, I had a history of crappy jobs that started at age 12 and continued well into my late twenties. My first crappy job was babysitting. Why any parent would leave me with a child, let alone multiple children, is beyond me. I was ill-suited for the endeavor, and I spent most of my time figuring out how to play video games instead. Next, I was a caddy. I knew nothing about golf; still don't. After that, I pulled weeds and laid mulch for a summer in the humid paradise of Chicago.

I could go on and on, but in truth, almost all of us have had (and some still have) crappy jobs that we wish we didn't have to do. But we do them anyway. Why? Because we want to take care of ourselves, and we have wants and needs. By the time children are old enough to learn about wants and needs, it's perfectly fine to make them work for some of their wants.

American children are bombarded with ads on TV, YouTube, and Facebook every day. Modern kids have a much longer "wants" list than average kids did a generation back. Targeted advertising, which works so well on adults, works equally well on children. This only fuels their appetite for consumption.

That's not a bad thing. Without wants or needs, there would be no motivation. Your child is motivated to work and earn, and that should be fostered. Good habits at a young age translate to good habits in adulthood. When a child works hard, saves money, and accomplishes a financial goal, they give themselves positive reinforcement. They will need this positive reinforcement as they plod through their crappy jobs in their early twenties.

The first set of crappy jobs, though, comes from inside the home. Every household inevitably has a laundry list (ha) of chores that need to be done at any given time: laundry, dishes, yardwork, pet care, and dusting, to name a few. Opportunities for age-appropriate chore assignments abound, and they are a great vehicle for implementing a rewards system. Having an hourly rate or a set payout per job facilitates a child's inventiveness and develops a strong work ethic.

When I was 12, my parents offered to pay me to babysit my sister. Many parents in my neighborhood felt that babysitting a younger sibling was more of a requirement and did not follow my parents' lead to sweeten the pot with cash. However, I was incentivized to make sure that she had a good time as I babysat. I was expected to play with her, keep her occupied, and of course, ensure her safety. If she told my parents that I locked her in her room and played Nintendo for three hours, I would not get paid or get hired again. So instead of doing that, I let my sister watch me play Nintendo for three hours. I was a boy genius.

Eventually, my parents found out about my less-than-stimulating child care technique. They didn't appreciate my ingenuity for concomitant video game playing and babysitting and yanked that job from me. I had officially been fired for the first time. Looking back, that was an important lesson in customer satisfaction. Due to poor performance, I lost a stream of income that was important to me and seriously hurt my Nintendo game acquisition ambitions.

It emphasized that a job done lazily results in no pay. This has held true throughout the entirety of my life, whether applied at the scholastic level or the working world. I can think of countless people I've encountered who have natural talent but lack motivation and discipline. I've seen it with athletics, academics, you name it. Despite their talents, they still are unable to forge ahead. Their attitude holds them back.

Two semi-famous Chicago athletes come to mind: Tom Waddle, one of my favorite Chicago Bears growing up, and William "Refrigerator" Perry. Waddle was a slow guy and a mediocre receiver at best, but he was fearless in the middle of the field. His career started in 1989 and ended in 1994, and I thought we'd never see him again. But Waddle worked hard to reinvent himself and learn new things, and now he has his own radio show and reports on football in Chicago.

The Fridge had a different story. In 1985, there was no bigger star than the Fridge. He scored a touchdown in the Super Bowl; he was the most famous, most recognizable athlete in Chicago. Like Tom Waddle, his career also ended in 1994. But the Fridge's story doesn't end as well as Tom Waddle's. The Fridge became penniless, and he nearly died because he didn't have the money to pay for a much-needed operation.

I'm not going to say the Fridge was lazy, because that isn't fair. I can say with certainty that the Fridge did not leverage his talents to the fullest extent possible. Compared to Tom Waddle on the football field, the Fridge had more talent in his right arm than Waddle in his entire body. But when their careers were over, Waddle chose a much different path and took his talents to the next level. Each man treated retirement in very different ways.

My approach to babysitting was like William Perry's. We both figured the good times were just going to roll. What could go wrong? When things did go wrong, we both ended up with no income. The difference is that William Perry had to support himself and his family, and my only consequence was having to play old video games. Better for me to learn that harsh lesson early than to learn it too late.

And that's what I'm trying to instill in my daughters. If you're going to sweep the floor, it has to be done right; otherwise, the job is not complete. While my eldest daughter may not have been that into the whole allowance thing, when she did do the work, she would always come and get me, and I would review it. Inevitably, she would miss some areas, and in order to get her $2, it would have to be done to my standard. Fingers crossed her first real boss is nicer than her dear old dad.

Check, Please!

Having kids is a wild, wonderful adventure and one that you can't fully plan for. However, as you begin to grow your family, keep the following points in mind so that you can stay on the right track financially and set your kids on their own financial path when the time comes.

1. **Kids are expensive.** Nothing can prepare you for having children—mentally, physically, or financially. Get used to not having a lot of excess cash, and say goodbye to the really cool vacations you used to take.

2. **Use the savings vehicles available to you wisely.** 529 Plans are used solely for college and have high contribution limits. An ESA has the benefit of being used for elementary and high school expenses. However, donors are limited to $2,000 of contributions every year, and a beneficiary cannot receive more than $2,000 in their ESA account cumulatively across all donors.

3. **As our online capabilities advance, education will change, and the economics of college will change as well.** College costs may start going down or leveling out at some point, but since that point is unknown, it's probably a good idea to keep saving.

4. **Teach money management to your children and start savings habits early.** Use a system such as GISS to have a structure that both you and your child can work with. The more you can teach delayed gratification now, the better off your kids will be in the future.

CHAPTER 5
Insurance: The Only Path to Hakuna Matata

My sister had a Disney movie addiction when we were kids. It started with The Little Mermaid in 1989, followed by Beauty and the Beast in 1991, and continued with Aladdin in 1992. I still have nightmares of watching those movies over and over again until both I and the VHS player were on the verge of breaking. I have most of the songs from that era of Disney memorized to this day.

Before I had children, I swore to my wife that we were not going to be a Disney princess family. Aside from the fact that I didn't want to relive my childhood of maddening Disney songs playing over and over and over again, I didn't like some of the Disney imagery of damsels in distress who needed to be saved by a prince. So for the first eighteen months of my eldest daughter's life, no princesses were allowed in my house.

Then came preschool, and as soon as my daughter saw a princess lunchbox, she was in love, and there was no going back. It is odd, however, watching these movies from an adult perspective. It's hard for me to turn off the risk-averse part of my brain and just enjoy watching the movie. In The Little Mermaid, Ariel doesn't have a mother, and she becomes separated from her family. Similarly, in Beauty and the Beast, Belle's mother dies when she is very young, and she is also separated from her father. Aladdin doesn't have parents at all, and Jasmine's mom is neither referenced nor depicted in the movie. What is going on here?

It doesn't stop there. As time has gone on, starting with The Lion King, these familial separations have become much more in-your-face and violent. We see Simba's dad trampled by wildebeests. Quasimodo is nearly throw into a well. Nemo's mom is eaten by a barracuda. And not only do Anna and Elsa's parents get swallowed by the sea, but we even see their subsequent funeral.

Disney movies scare the crap out of not only my kids but me as well. They make me uncomfortable and force me to consider my own mortality and face other possibilities that could have a tremendous impact on my family. What if I, too, am trampled by wildebeests? As a father of three, I really have to contemplate how to protect my family against the effects of an untimely demise.

In this chapter, we'll discuss different kinds of insurance you can use to protect yourself in case of attack by barracuda, wildebeest, ocean liner, or other incidents leading to unplanned death or severe health-care costs.

Bad Health, Bad Wealth: Examining Health Insurance Options

Health gets in the way of a lot. Bad health can crush your financial present and future. Not only does it inhibit one's ability to earn, but it also generates bills and puts major stress on family dynamics.

The number one reason why my pre-retiree clients are postponing retirement is health insurance. Many don't want to switch to private insurance for fear they will have to change doctors. Additionally, the added cost for private health insurance, which can run in excess of $25,000 a year per couple, may be a financial impossibility to take on. And that doesn't include co-pays, deductibles, or co-insurance.

Even for my clients who are just starting out or in their prime working years, there is significant concern about health insurance. Employers often have a few different plans to choose from. The most common types are PPOs, HMOs, and many times those types of plans qualify for HSAs. Each plan has its own unique features, and some even come with serious tax benefits to boot.

First off, there is some basic terminology that we should lay out. The following table lists common insurance-related terms and what they mean for you:

Term	Definition
Premium	The amount you have to pay, typically monthly, to have the insurance coverage.
Deductible	An out-of-pocket amount you must pay before your insurance kicks in.
Co-pay	An amount you pay every time you set foot into a doctor's office regardless of deductibles.
Co-insurance	The percentage you are responsible for after you hit the deductible, up to a certain amount
Maximum out-of-pocket	The most you have to pay (excluding co-pays) between your deductible and co-insurance.

HMOs (Health Maintenance Organizations) are where the whole health insurance regime, as we know it, started. Under an HMO, a patient's medical decisions all start at the general practitioner level. This means the primary care physician (PCP) acts as the gatekeeper for the insurance company. If the patient is having stomach problems and wants to see a gastrointestinal specialist, they have to get a referral from their primary care doctor first.

Because people are required to get a referral, they tend to use specialists less often, and since they use specialists less often, the insurance company charges less for an HMO typically. Of course, the downside is that the patient loses a certain level of control. If they really want to see a gastroenterologist for a problem, their PCP may tell them no, and there is little recourse.

PPOs (Preferred Provider Organizations) are built upon the HMO model, but instead of making a patient go through their PCP, the patient can choose to see a specialist on their own. This gives the patient freedom to choose when to go to specialists. This means patients also have the freedom to run up large medical bills based upon a whim or irrational fear. This makes PPOs more expensive.

The list of doctors that a PPO user can see does have limits. Some doctors are in-network; others are out-of-network. Visiting an in-network doctor gives you the most bang for your buck. Although in-network specialists typically have higher co-pays than PCPs, you can save yourself from surprise bills. If you go out-of-network, you may find that a large portion of what the doctor charged is not covered by your insurance and what is covered by your insurance is subject to higher co-insurance payments and higher out-of-pocket maximums.

HSAs (Health Spending Accounts) are a feature of some types of insurance plans known as High Deductible Health Plans (HDHP). HMOs and PPOs both have deductibles. (Remember, this is the amount you are responsible to pay before insurance kicks in.) They can range from $250 to $1,000 for individuals. Similarly, maximum out-of-pockets have a wide range as well. An HDHP is a type of plan that has at least a $1,300 deductible for individuals ($2,600 for families), with a maximum out-of-pocket of $6,550 and $13,100 respectively (in 2017).

The benefit of having such a plan is that the insured can use an HSA to pay for health care expenses. If you are funding your HSA from your paycheck, the contribution is pre-tax. This account can be funded up to $3,400 for an individual plan, or $6,750 for a family plan (for 2017). Some banks pay a good amount of interest, but the money also has the potential to be invested in the market. Another great feature is that the money can be carried forward without limitation—there is no "use it or lose it" at the end of each year.

As previously mentioned, whatever someone puts into their plan, they get to deduct on their tax return (or not include in income). But wait, there's more. Whatever is taken out and used for qualified medical expenses comes out tax-free. This is one of the only accounts where you get to double-dip. The first dip is the deduction, and the second dip is taking out the earnings sans tax. At this point you're saying to yourself, "Yeah, but the deductibles are huge." You're right, they are, which is why I would not do it...now.

I did have an HSA account when my wife and I first got married. We were young, healthy people with no kids, and we just didn't go to the doctor all that often. It was fantastic. Low insurance premiums with an incredible tax savings vehicle can't be beat. What happened? Kids. Once we had kids, going to the doctor was a monthly event, and the HSA wasn't worth it for the higher deductible and max out-of-pocket.

Because of the high deductibles, the premiums are lower, which makes HDHPs alluring and increasingly common. Millennials can really take advantage of this. Many of us are choosing to get married and have children later on in life, or sometimes not at all. This means that tax-free money can be saved, invested, and held until needed. Of course, taking a lot of market risk on money you need for paying medical bills may not be the best idea, so invest wisely.

What About Your Stuff?

Every day in California, nearly every person between the ages of 22 and 65 jumps into a piece of metal and goes screaming down an interstate at speeds in excess of 70 to 80 miles per hour. Despite the fact we don't think twice about this incredibly dangerous activity, many of us eat, smoke, text, and Facebook while driving, and some even do it under the influence of drugs or alcohol. This is insane. Driving a car is by far the most dangerous thing you'll do in your life, assuming you don't BASE jump regularly. You can cause immeasurable damage, not only to yourself but also to others and their property. This is a tremendous amount of liability.

How do you protect your assets? Through insurance, of course.

Car Insurance

You can use auto insurance to protect against others and protect against yourself. When protecting yourself against the world (meaning other than an accident with another car), you'll typically use something called comprehensive insurance. Someone spray paints your car, hail destroys your hood, you hit a cow in the middle of the road—that is all covered by comprehensive insurance. If it is an accident between two cars, that is covered by collision insurance.

Like health insurance, both comprehensive and collision insurance have deductibles, which is the amount you are responsible for before the insurance company will start paying. This can range from $250 to $2,000. Like health insurance, the higher the deductible, the lower the premium. Taking the $2,000 deductible is placing a bet on yourself that you are a good driver (and a lucky one) who won't get in an accident. Remember, if you are hit by someone who doesn't have insurance, your insurance company will still pay for your repairs under collision coverage, but you'll be out the whole $2,000 deductible in one go, unless you have uninsured coverage (to be discussed shortly).

Property is not the only concern in an automobile accident and comes in a distant second to personal injury. Serious injury or death is where the bulk of damages occur. When injured, a person can be compensated for their out-of-pocket medical expenses, pain and suffering, lost wages...and the list goes on and on.

The problem of the uninsured motorist again rears its ugly head. In order to get paid out for a collision with an uninsured driver, you need to have uninsured coverage. With uninsured coverage, you can get paid out for your claim by your insurance company in the same way as if it were coming from the other driver.

The important part is knowing your coverages and how to read an insurance statement. Your insurance company will send you a declarations page for your policy (called a "deck sheet" in the industry). The deck sheet is going to break down all the coverage you have. Every state requires some amount of personal liability insurance. This is the insurance to cover the damages that you may cause. Not having personal liability insurance is against the law.

Personal liability is usually shown as two numbers: smaller/bigger. The smaller number is the per person liability coverage you have per accident. So, if the smaller number is $250,000, every person involved in an accident where you are at fault can claim a maximum of $250,000 in damages. The bigger number is the maximum the insurance company will pay per accident. If that number is $500,000, then all victims combined can claim no more than that amount in damages.

Here's an example using $250,000/$500,000. You run a red light and T-bone a minivan with two adults and two kids in the car. Adult 1 has $100,000 of damage, adult two has $265,000 of damage, Child 1 has $70,000 of damage, and Child 2 has $90,000 worth of damage. Adult Two will not have their claim of $265,000 entirely fulfilled because it is $15,000 above the maximum of $250,000 per individual. The combined claims from the rest of the victims add up to $260,000. That totals $510,000, which is $10,000 above the $500,000 combined limit, which means the insurance company won't pay the full amount claimed; they will only pay $500,000. Does that mean the remaining $25,000 in claims goes away? No. In this case, you are responsible for an out-of-pocket payment for the remaining $25,000.

So what happens if you hit a school bus full of children? Bad things. That's why you buy umbrella coverage. An umbrella policy will pay an additional amount should a really bad accident happen. Typically, umbrella policies start at $1 million of additional coverage, but it is not uncommon to have a $5 million policy. Plan on spending around $300 per year for a $1 million umbrella and an additional $150 for each additional million dollars of coverage.

How much of an umbrella should you have? Figure enough to cover your assets. If you only have $50 to your name and own no property, having an umbrella is not super important. If you have a horrible accident, you'll probably end up filing for bankruptcy, and as long as you didn't intentionally hit the bus, you may end up having the damages discharged. Consult a bankruptcy attorney before taking any actions. Also, put down your burger/vape/iPhone and don't hit a school bus. Plus, people who vape look stupid. (You can thank me later.)

Homeowners Insurance or Renters Insurance

While your car may be your greatest liability, your greatest asset is your home. This means that homeowners insurance is a must. Not only does your mortgage company require you to maintain homeowners insurance, but it just makes sense. The homeowners policy is split into a few different parts that cover different areas of your home. I'll talk about California policies, but different states are going to have different rules.

The first part is called dwelling coverage, which covers the home itself. The amount of coverage is not the fair market value of the home, but rather the replacement cost. Replacement cost is how much money it will take to rebuild the home. If you have an upgraded kitchen, you're going to want to bake that into the replacement cost. Almost all policies have an extended amount of around 10%. This means that the insurance company will pay an additional 10% of the dwelling coverage, just in case the replacement cost estimate ends up being low.

One mistake that homeowners make is including the 10% additional coverage as part of the insurable amount of the house. This is a bad idea. The 10% amount is a backstop. Think about it like a balcony railing on a high-rise building. The railing runs up to the edge of the balcony to keep people safe. Some morons on YouTube decide that the railing is just another part of the balcony and will do handstands on it, hang off of it, or do all sorts of stupid stuff. Once you get past the balcony there is nothing left to save you, and once you get past the 10% additional coverage, the insurance company stops paying.

The second part is called extensions. Things like detached garages, fencing, or even a treehouse would be covered as an extension. This is usually set at 10% of the dwelling coverage.

The third part covers personal property. This is all of your stuff: clothing, couches, desks, chairs, or anything not permanently affixed to the house itself. You usually get 75% of your dwelling coverage for personal property. It's important to know that not all property is covered 100%. Jewelry, guns, antiques, and cash all have single-item limits and combined limits. If you have any extensive collection or artwork, you may need a special policy called a floater.

Many policies include a loss of use clause, so that if you must leave your home for repairs, the insurance company will pay for a hotel room up to a certain period of time (usually a year to 24 months). The other important part of a policy is the deductible. Since you'll likely only use your policy if something really big happens, you may as well keep the deductible high, which will make the premium lower.

If you're a renter, you also need to have insurance. Because you don't have an ownership interest in the home, you don't need to worry about the structure itself—that's the landlord's concern. Your stuff is your concern, and you need a renters policy. These policies are typically inexpensive, and depending on the quality (and quantity) of things you have, you may only need $25,000, but it's better to have too much than not enough.

Life Insurance: Stomped by a Wildebeest

For a brief time I was an insurance agent with Farmers Insurance. My regional director (RD) told me a story that I have never forgotten and that has impacted my decision-making greatly when it comes to insurance. My RD came from an insurance family, and had a number of brothers and sisters. His father was a successful agent, and eventually most of the family went into insurance.

But the RD's father passed away in his thirties when most of the kids (including the RD) were still very young. Did the insurance salesman father have any life insurance on his own life? Not a single dollar. So for years the family struggled, and eventually many of the children went into the insurance business for themselves. But think of the suffering that the family went through. It's horrific to lose your father at a young age, but also losing income and stability is potentially catastrophic.

Life insurance is not a want; it is a need. Moreover, most people I speak to have a tendency to underestimate the amount of insurance they require. In my mind, when life insurance is in question, it is better to have too much than not enough. This is especially true when it comes to term (often referred to as "temporary") life insurance, where the price per $1,000 of benefit is minimal.

If I Had a DIME...

There is a mnemonic that helps calculate the correct level of insurance for a couple: DIME. DIME stands for Debt, Income, Mortgage, and Education.

Debt

Debt is what you owe aside from your mortgage. The most common debt that I always ask about is credit card debt, but it also includes student debt and auto loans. Do you want to saddle your loved ones with this debt? The debt does not simply go away when you do. While the dead person may be the one who signed for the loan, the company holding the debt has a claim against the estate. The trustee, usually the surviving spouse, has an obligation to pay off all outstanding debts.

Income

Income means replacing the income of the deceased individual. If a person does not have a family to support, then this is moot. Many clients have told me that since they work inside the home, there is no need for replacement income. Wrong! The value of services of someone who works inside the home is, to some extent, immeasurable. Think of all of the services that person provides: caring for children, driving children to school and other appointments, cooking, cleaning, sometimes paying the bills, being at home for deliveries, clothes shopping, food shopping, help at night with children...and the list, as my wife can attest to, does not end.

The question becomes, how much income to replace? This is a sticky question. I have spoken to many couples about this with varying results. It really boils down to priorities. For deceased primary wage earners, oftentimes they'll say that their surviving spouses can get a job and offset some loss of income. This is a faulty notion, especially early on. The week after losing their spouse/ parent of their children, the last thing they want to do is go job hunting. It may be a couple of years or more before the surviving spouse will want to think about dusting off their résumé.

There is also a tendency for people to think that they should not replace their monthly savings. That is, they claim that because they only spend $5,000 a month, the replacement should be based off that amount rather than the $10,000 per month they actually earn. Again, this is wrong. Replacing savings is equally important. The primary wage earner would have retired at some point, and the savings would be for retirement. Similarly, the insurance money needs to cover not only current expenses but also at least a portion of the surviving spouse's retirement.

Other times, couples will assume that the person will remarry and there will not be a need for a lot of income. Really, is that what you want? You decide to replace five years of income, and by Year 4 your spouse starts to desperately seek someone to marry. I'd rather have my spouse focus on my children and not have to worry about marrying for survival.

When I advise clients, I typically tell them to cover the other spouse's income or household value up until the kids will likely be in high school. The rationale is that for the spouse working inside the home, when the kids get to a certain age they will be self-sufficient (enough) that the surviving spouse will have more options..

Mortgage
The biggest financial undertaking that families make in their lifetimes is their personal residence. With that personal residence usually comes a mortgage, and if you live in California, that mortgage ranges from sizeable all the way to obscene. While being able to pay off the mortgage can be considered a budgetary measure (a decrease in expenses), that's not the only reason to give one's spouse the ability to own the residence free and clear.

In my mind, if I leave my spouse a free and clear home, she doesn't have to feel the pressure of moving. I know that if I die unexpectedly the whole family will be in upheaval, and giving my spouse enough money to own the house outright makes me sleep better at night. My children will always have a place to live, and that means a lot to me. Tack on my income replacement, and my kids through age eighteen will be comfortable.

Education

The last part of our mnemonic is education. I previously mentioned that Yale will cost $150,000 per year by the year 2030, or around $600,000 for four years. Despite this reality, I have never advised a client to take out $600,000 in insurance per child for education. What I usually recommend is that we take the current-year value of Yale, multiply by four, and say that if one spouse dies unexpectedly, we'll invest and hopefully keep up with inflation.

This rule of thumb is not without caveats. If a parent with a newborn child takes out a 20-year policy and a parent dies in Year 10, the face amount of the policy has not gone up, but Yale's tuition has. Furthermore, the investment period is not eighteen years any longer, but rather eight. What this means is that the child may not be able to go to Yale, or perhaps has to take on student loans, which is not ideal, but will cover the gap in tuition.

What does this all functionally mean? First, the 2015 average mortgage in the U.S. is around $295,000. Yale costs around $260,000 for four years, which means that on average, without any provision for replacement of income, a family of four should have at least $815,000 of life insurance per working parent as a bare minimum. Tack on replacement of income, and that number is going to shoot up well above a million dollars quite easily and likely should be closer to two million.

Pick Your Poison, er...Policy Type

Now that we've calculated the amount of insurance needed with DIME, the next step is picking what kind of policy you want. There are basically two: permanent and term.

A permanent insurance policy is designed to last for a person's lifetime. Typically, the policy carries a cash value. This means the policy can be surrendered (given up) and the insurance company will pay you the cash inside the policy. As long as you pay the cost of the insurance, the permanent policy will never go away.

Term insurance, on the other hand, is designed to end at a particular time. A term policy has no cash value, so once you no longer want the policy you stop paying the premiums and the insurance lapses. Term insurance typically lasts ten, twenty, or thirty years. Should you want to continue coverage after the term ends, you'll have to get a new policy and get your health reevaluated.

The main driver of cost in both types of insurance is health. The insurance company does not want to take a risk on an unhealthy person unless they are adequately compensated. The most important factor is the height-to-weight ratio, which is basically body mass index (BMI). A bad BMI will yield a bad table. A table is a schedule of premiums for a subset of people with a particular level of risk. The better your table, the better your rates. Insurance companies will also look at blood pressure, urinalysis, cholesterol, and other health metrics.

They will also look at your health history. If you've had any major diseases, such as cancer or an autoimmune disorder, plan on having a difficult time obtaining insurance. Smoking will also dramatically increase your rates. Less obvious, if you had a parent who died young from a heart attack or cancer, you will likely not get the best rates the insurance company has to offer.

The final factor that drives premium, which is often overlooked, is the frequency that the premium payments are made. The cheapest method is annual. By paying the premium in one lump sum annually, the owner can get the best deal. Next best is semiannual. Most insurance companies will tack on a minimal charge for semiannual payments. Typically, the most expensive way to pay is monthly. Before you agree to monthly payments, figure out how much it's really going to cost.

Object/Insurance Permanence

When babies are born, they have a simplistic view of the world. They cry, they eat, and they poop. It's the simple life, really. But part of that simplicity is believing that once something disappears it is gone forever; this is called object permanence. When Mom leaves the room, baby thinks Mom is gone forever. This principal rears its head within the context of insurance as well.

Even though permanent insurance is a variant of insurance unto itself, there are three sub-variations that are often presented to would-be purchasers:

- » Whole life
- » Variable life
- » Universal life

All three have their own unique attributes, but they share a couple of similarities. First, they all are non-cancellable (except for cases where the insured does not pay their premium). This means that if for some reason the insured gets sick, the insurance company cannot raise the premium or cancel the policy on that basis.

Next, all the variations have some sort of cash value. This means that when the owner pays the premium, part of that payment is held within the policy, at least in the beginning. Cash value means that you can do some interesting things with an insurance policy. Usually, an owner can remove the cash and put it somewhere else. The cash can sit in the account and earn some stated rate of interest. Owners can even take a loan out from the policy.

This can be a double-edged sword at times. First, there are tax rules and implications that occur when the owner starts to play with the cash value of an insurance account. Second, there is often a surrender period in which, for a certain period of time at the beginning of the policy (sometimes as long as eight years), there is a penalty for withdrawing from the account. Third, any amount taken (except for a loan) in excess of the premiums deposited will be taxed as ordinary income. Loans are not free, and interest is accrued while the loan is outstanding. Thankfully, most times the dividends in the policy will cover the loan interest. Additionally, most policies today also have no-lapse provisions which protect a policy from collapsing due to interest payments from loans.

If the loan and interest are not paid back by the time of death, the death benefit to the beneficiary is reduced. The nuances of cash value aside, the distinctions between the three main varieties of permanent insurance begin to unfold.

Let's dive into whole life insurance, which is the conservative grandpa of the group. Tried and true, old reliable, there aren't many surprises with whole life. There is an interest rate stated up front, that interest rate is credited at near a constant rate, and the person keeps paying their premium until they die or no longer want the policy. There is always a guaranteed rate, which is the minimum, but the rate can rise as the insurance company makes more money. In the 1980s, interest rates rose significantly, but more recently, that rate has been fairly low. The policies are set to never fail, so there are no surprises unless the insurance company goes belly up.

Variable life insurance is the crazy stockbroker brother-in-law. For some people, insurance just isn't exciting enough, and money sitting in a cash account earning some set percentage is boring. Variable life allows a person to invest in some kind of mutual fund so that their cash value grows (or falls) at a greater (and more unpredictable) rate. At first blush, this isn't necessarily a bad deal. The owner may have this policy for decades, and given that markets generally go up over time, it seemingly makes sense since the money isn't really going anywhere anyway.

The first problem is that if the market takes a major downturn, your policy may end up being underfunded. The typical owner of a permanent policy usually does not pay much attention to this, but sure enough, over the life of the policy it will show less going into the cash account, which means more is going to the cost of insurance. Under whole life, market fluctuations don't matter because premiums are calculated based upon an interest rate. However, with variable life, if an insured lives long enough and the market performs poorly enough, this premium may not be able to fund the cost of insurance. When that happens, the insufficiency is taken out of the cash value of the policy. If that happens over a long period of time, the policy can be bankrupted, which means the premiums can't cover the costs, and there is not cash value: the proverbial double whammy.

But that isn't the part about variable life insurance that irks me the most. What I don't like are the investment choices. It's not that the quality of choices is necessarily bad, but all the baggage that comes along with the choices makes insurance policies a bad investment. When invested in a variable life policy, the insurance company is not going to let the owner pick any investments that you want, but rather the investments that the insurance company has on their menu. Insurance companies are like restaurants. They have a set menu of options, and if you don't like it, go to a different restaurant. This means that, like restaurants, they get to charge what they want, and they get a good chunk of whatever is invested in the fund.

Insurance companies will even partner with well-known investment companies to help entice the owner to use that fund. The problem is that not only will the investment company get their pound of flesh, but the insurance company will put an additional layer of expense on top of the investment and collect an additional fee for itself. There are some lower cost investment options out there, but they are rare, and you need to examine your options and the total cost of the proposed policy costs very carefully.

These costs are ever-present, and can be upwards of 2%. Thus, there is a high bar to get decent returns. With an internal cost of 2%, you don't make a penny until the market crosses that threshold. So from my perspective, if you have the insurance because you need it, why put the cash reserves at risk of depletion by a fickle market?

The last option for permanent life insurance is universal life. Universal life sort of marries whole life and variable life. It has a stated interest rate like that of whole life, but that interest rate can fluctuate. The fluctuations are not as wild as the movements in a variable life policy but, nevertheless, offer an opportunity to grow the cash balance in the account faster than that of whole life.

Universal life also has some nice flexibility. The owner of the policy is able to stop premiums altogether as long as there is sufficient cash within the policy to pay for it. Interest rates can vary widely, so unlike a whole life policy, should the interest rate stay low long enough, there is a possibility that the policy will bankrupt.

Note: The important lesson to remember about permanent policies relates back to the object permanence discussion. In a universal life policy, even though the premium may disappear or go down, that doesn't mean that your policy is in good shape. In fact, it often means the opposite. With variable life, just because your premium remains level in a down market, that doesn't mean that your policy is doing well. Caveat emptor always applies, and if it looks too good to be true, it probably is.

The Case for Term-ites

Insurance is one of the most important tools in the personal finance toolkit. I have several policies on my own life since I want to make sure my family is taken care of in the event that I die unexpectedly. It's not as easy as just buying insurance, though; you still have to make sure the insurance company isn't taking you for a ride.

I mentioned before that I trained as a captive insurance agent for a bit. It was an interesting view into a world that I knew very little about. My regional manager was an awesome salesman. If I could channel 10% of his skill, I'd be on the cover of some swanky investment magazine.

During one of my trainings on life insurance, this manager warned me about "term-ites." A term-ite is an agent who sells term life insurance almost exclusively. Insurance companies typically want to sell their full range of insurance, and not just term life, so they often award much better commissions to their agents when they sell permanent insurance. In selling to potential clients, we are trained to take the angle that an insurance policy makes a great savings account, and the money is tax-deferred.

The reality is that permanent insurance is neither a great savings account, nor is it really that great at tax deferral. It is great at forcing people to save...most times. The way it works is that the premium payment is bifurcated into cost of insurance and cash value. As people get older, the cost of the life insurance tends to go up. This is not a big problem because early on in the policy, less of the premium goes to cost of insurance, more goes to cash value, and there is compound interest earned on the cash value.

Because insurance companies pay more than the typical bank (the owner of the policy may get 2% or more), even in really low-interest environments, this can look like a great deal. But in order to get that great deal, you need to buy the insurance product, which is where insurance companies make their money. In the end, the interest ends up being an all-to-familiar loss leader product. They make a lot of money on the insurance and pay you a portion through the interest they credit. They also get to invest the money that you pay them, which means they get interest on your cash value over and above the money they make from the insurance product.

From a tax deferral standpoint, permanent insurance is also problematic. It does indeed defer tax, which I am all for. But the wrapper around the tax deferral is an insurance product, and there will be a time in an insured's life where the insurance is no longer necessary (old age, change in financial situation, etc.). The issue is that when you want to unwind the contract, you have to pay the tax to do so. You can exchange it tax-free, but only for another insurance policy or an annuity. However, if you want the cash, there will be tax due on earnings applied at ordinary tax rates.

Because of these reasons, I am a "term-ite" and proud of it. The whole purpose of life insurance is to protect against the loss of income. If an investor wants to save money for a rainy day, I would advise them to use a bank account. If an investor wants to invest, I would advise them to use a brokerage account. Insurance, like investments, should be done as cheaply as possible.

Term policies are cheap, relative to permanent insurance. They get the job done without many frills. As I noted before, health drives premium. For term insurance, the other big factor is the duration of the insurance. Term insurance is guaranteed for a limited period of time. The most common periods are 10, 15, 20, and 30 years. The longer the term, the higher the premium. More years means more opportunity for the insured to die. The mortality rate amongst humans is 100%. Time remains undefeated.

However, my clients often have a concern about what happens if they get sick towards the end of the policy and have a shorter life expectancy. Thankfully, most insurance carriers have what is called a conversion clause. What that means is that, at any point during the policy, a term policy can be converted to a permanent policy. Will the premium go up? Yes. The insurance company will make you start premiums at the age at which you convert. So if you purchased the policy at age 18 and are 47 when you want to convert, you should prepare for some serious sticker shock.

However, the insurance company, generally, will not re-rate the insured for health. This means that even if a person gets sick and is likely to die sooner rather than later, he or she can extend that term insurance policy by converting it to permanent insurance without poor health being a factor.

You've Lost Your Leg, Now What? Long-Term Disability

What would happen if you suddenly became so ill that you couldn't work? What if that meant you couldn't pay your bills? Who would feed and clothe your children? The answer is, at least in part, Social Security. Part of the function of Social Security is to help disabled people survive through a series of payments. Perhaps Social Security can take care of some of a family's needs, but it certainly cannot cover all expenses. Thankfully, insurance companies have a solution for this. It's called long-term disability (LTD), and in my experience, it is one of the most underutilized insurance products on the market.

I actually have a passion for LTD. A close friend of mine was diagnosed with multiple sclerosis in her early thirties. It happened to be a particularly aggressive form of MS, and only a few years after she was diagnosed, she was forced to retire from her work. She didn't have any children, but she did have a mortgage, and she had to support herself.

She was a planner, believed heavily in insurance, and had purchased an LTD policy back when almost nobody had even heard of it. She saved her own financial life. Her decision to purchase LTD allowed her to stay in her house, pay for medical treatment, and cover her other living expenses with no income from work. She absolutely leveraged Social Security and Medicare, but without the additional money coming in every month from the policy, her future would have been uncertain.

Most states have mechanisms to cover a person for a short period of time, perhaps three to six months, but to cover a long-term disability takes an insurance product. These products usually kick in after some period of time called an elimination period. This waiting period can be as short as three months or as long as a year. They can pay out for a period of years, until the person reaches 65, or continue on in perpetuity.

LTD policies have interesting tax benefits. Policies that are purchased with after-tax funds pay out in after-tax money. Pre-tax policies pay out pre-tax. What this means is that if you are receiving an LTD policy from an employer through payroll deductions and are not being taxed on the value of the policy currently, should the LTD policy pay out, you will owe tax on that money at ordinary rates. If the policy value is being taxed or the taxpayer is paying outside of payroll, that benefit will be tax-free.

An insured person will want to cover as much of his income as possible. It is important to be aware that many companies will only allow a person to cover two-thirds of their current income. They also talk to one another, so double-dipping is not an option. If a person becomes partially disabled, they will receive their benefit amount less what they are able to make, as replacement of income.

Probably the most important clause in the long-term disability contract is the definition of "disability." This definition of "disability" drives how much a person can collect on the policy, if anything at all. Most people think that since they can't work their normal job ("own occupation"), they are entitled to their full disability payment. Unfortunately, this is often not the case. There also exists a concept of "any occupation," where the person is expected to take on some level of employment, even it is not the work the insured was used to doing.

There are, however, some disabilities which are presumed to be total disabilities, leaving the person unable to do work of any kind. These ailments typically include loss of sight in both eyes, loss of hearing in both ears, loss of speech, loss of use of both hands, loss of use of both feet, and loss of use of one hand and one foot. Even if the person can return to work, the policy will continue to pay out.

Long-Term Care, Closer Than You Think (CODA)

Long-term disability helps people replace lost income as the result of not being able to work. Long-term care (LTC) helps people pay for medical care that is either not covered by insurance, is partially covered by insurance, or is only covered for a short period of time. Most of the time, long-term care pertains to the elderly. However, with more cases of early onset Alzheimer's, MS, and ALS, young people are occasionally affected. The problem is that Medicare has strict rules as to what counts as Medicare eligible. The care has to be medical care, and nursing care does not count as medical. Having someone in your house assist with tasks also does not count. The LTC policy is a way to pay for such expenses. An insured becomes eligible to use an LTC policy when he or she is unable to complete two of the six activities of daily living without assistance: bathing, dressing, toileting, eating, walking, and incontinence.

When you purchase an LTC policy, you pay a premium, just like any other insurance policy. The amount of LTC you want drives the cost of your premium. LTC payouts can range from $150 per day all the way up to $500 per day. Oftentimes, there are riders offered, which allow for waiver of premium once the benefit starts, or riders that increase the benefit with inflation over the life of the policy. Like LTD, there is also an elimination or waiting period, typically six months but can be as much as a year.

Back in the day, when LTC policies first came out, they were relatively simple. The insured would pay a premium, and the insurance company would pay a certain amount every month for as long as the person needed it with no limit. That simplicity has been thrown to the wolves, and an unlimited benefit period is almost never used. Many companies that had such contracts in place have been allowed by the states to either amend the terms of the policies or dramatically increase premiums midstream.

The duration of the benefit also has a big impact on the premium. The longer an insured wants the benefit to pay out, the more expensive the policy. Despite these two factors being the biggest driver of premiums, health plays an important role yet again. It is more expensive for a cancer survivor or elderly person to pick up a long-term care policy.

Choosing the amount of the benefit is probably the most difficult part of the policy selection process. We can know how much LTC benefit is needed in today's dollars, and we can use riders or estimate future cost to make sure the rate of payout is appropriate. But the length of the benefit period is ultimately asking you to predict how long LTC payouts will be needed. It's an impossible task. My professional recommendation for relatively healthy people in their fifties or sixties is at least $300 per day with an inflation rider; if you are not interested in an inflation rider, then increase that amount to $350 or $400. For younger people, it's wise to make it $300 per day, but having an inflation rider is a must. Make sure the policy pays out for at least 24 months.

The biggest problem that I see with LTC policies is that there are so many flavors with so many twists and variations, it is often difficult to discern one policy from the next. Some policies offer full in-home care coverage, some none. A lot of newer policies are offering a life insurance and LTC combo. If you die before you end up using your LTC benefits, your family gets some life insurance amount. These will be more costly than traditional LTC policies, and you need to examine both the life and LTC benefits carefully.

Bottom line: When it comes to LTC policies, working with a professional who knows the products is crucial.

Check, Please!

Now that you're sufficiently freaked out about everything that could go wrong in your life, take a deep breath and just remember the following key points to protect yourself as much as possible:

1. **Don't skimp on insurance because when you really need it, it needs to be sufficient.** Make sure you have enough to cover your potential losses.

2. **Life insurance is a crucial part of everyone's financial plan, but don't over-buy life insurance.** A lot of insurance agents have drunk their own Kool-Aid and really think that you should drink it too. Permanent insurance has very specific uses. If your main concern is providing for your family through college, term insurance will usually do the trick—and for a very reasonable price.

3. **Be conservative in your estimates.** Use the DIME method
   to figure out what you think your family's needs are; then tack on an
   additional $500,000. If using term insurance, the additional coverage
   will not be cost prohibitive, and it's better to be a little over-insured
   than under-insured.

4. **Death isn't the only thing to be afraid of; you must also
   consider protecting your family with long-term care and
   long-term disability insurance.** Many people will end up in a
   long-term scenario and will spend a great deal of their assets on their
   care rather than using that money to take care of their families.

5. **Choose your health insurance wisely.** Young, healthy couples or individuals should strongly consider an HSA to maximize their
   tax advantages. Families or those with less fortunate health should
   probably look harder at traditional health plans because the deductibles will likely be lower.

6. **Make sure your gear is adequately insured.** Your home,
   your stuff, and your car are all important components of your financial life. Make sure that you have them covered. Use higher deductibles to lower premiums.

CHAPTER 6

Investing the Non-Stupid Way

I'm a huge sports fan, and I don't really care about the actual sport involved when watching. Football, baseball, hockey, soccer, golf, rugby, curling, archery, or even competitive hacky-sack, if there is sports clickbait to be found, I'm clicking on it. I'll even gladly sit through the eternity known as a 30-second ad. (I can't believe I made it through full-on commercial breaks during childhood.)

Being a financial advisor, I am particularly aware of the ads relating to investing. You see ads on the Internet and television about gold, ETFs, and various mutual funds. They use people's insecurities to stir up emotions. Whether it's beating the market or keeping one's money intact during a down market, a seemingly endless stream of Wall Street "experts" have the answers to whatever ails you.

To put it bluntly, the conventional Wall Street way of investing is a fool's errand. Stock picking has little to no value. Hedge funds are scary, expensive, and only available to a fraction of investors. But if the way Wall Street tells you to invest doesn't make any sense, then how should you invest? First, stop asking Wall Street. They make all their money selling products and creating noise to confuse investors. Second, start listening to academia. Their message is clear and unencumbered:

1. Diversify.

2. Take risks only if compensated.

In this chapter, we'll go through some of the basics of diversification. Wall Street has sold the idea of diversification to investors but with little explanation of what a well-diversified portfolio might look like. We'll also unpack some of the different kinds of risks that investors take when investing in the bond or stock market and which risks are the ones worth taking. Finally, we'll talk about using advisors versus going it alone.

Diversify, Diversify, Diversify

Almost every advisor tells their clients to "diversify." The problem is many fail to explain why diversification is important, and every advisor has a different definition of "diversification." This isn't terribly surprising. Financial advisors work exclusively with numbers, and with enough torture, numbers will say anything you want them to.

However, truth does exist. To understand the nature of diversification and why it works, we need to travel to the past and visit with a post-WWII graduate student by the name of Harry Markowitz. In 1955, while Markowitz was studying economics, he had a chance conversation with a fellow grad student about his dissertation and decided to explore applying mathematical methods to stock prices. (Check out http://www.nobelprize.org/nobel_prizes/economic-sciences/laureates/1990/markowitz-bio.html if you're interested.)

As he ran numbers and tried out different theories, Markowitz discovered something phenomenal. As the number of asset classes increased, so did the returns. More importantly, the risk, as measured by volatility, decreased. When volatility decreases, the portfolio does not fluctuate as much. This flew in the face of conventional wisdom, which encouraged a handful of high-performing individual stocks. Markowitz knew the belief that stocks were priced by the expected future dividend payout was flawed.

Markowitz had discovered modern portfolio theory (MPT). The premise of this theory is that the more uncorrelated or negatively correlated stocks a portfolio has, the better the return and the lower the volatility. This fact is now well known to all MBA and undergraduate finance students. By extension, this means it is also well known to all mutual fund managers.

Consider sectors. Sectors are a group of mostly very tightly correlated stocks. (Think oil and gas, technology, health care and life sciences, etc.) While things like business risk (that a single company may make bad decisions that lead to its downfall) may not be an issue because the pool is so big, negative news for an industry can affect all stocks within that industry. So in 2001, when the dot-com boom busted and the world lost faith in high-tech companies being able to turn a profit, the whole thing unraveled. There was no safe tech company, so Nicholas, Janus, and all the other mutual funds concentrated in high-tech stocks took it in the shorts just like everybody else.

Strangely, when investors or managers pick stocks, they tend to choose stocks with close correlations. They will often stick with large cap U.S. stocks or emerging markets stocks. However, the effects are the same. When a particular asset class is overemphasized and that asset class takes a dip, the results can be catastrophic. Thanks to Markowitz, we now know there is a logical explanation for it.

How to diversify can be tricky. Many people (and experts) feel that they can diversify using individual stocks. Many come into my office with a hundred or so stocks thinking they have done a good job at diversifying their portfolio. Unfortunately, they are wrong. Most times, the stocks are almost entirely in the S&P 500, meaning they are all U.S. large companies. There is no international exposure, and no small exposure. Given the universe of securities is well over 10,000, an individual investor simply can't use individual stocks to diversify because of the trading cost.

Open-end mutual funds provide a good method of diversification. In an open-end mutual fund, when new money is added, the company creates more shares. The new money is used to purchase more securities inside of the fund. The fund is therefore valued at its net asset value (NAV). Since adding shares creates more shares and redeeming takes shares away, the flow of money has no impact on the share price.

Closed-end mutual funds are much more like stocks. They start out with an investment period, but once they close, they no longer accept more money into the fund. The only way to buy shares is to buy them from another investor. This means that price of the fund can be greater or lesser than the price of the underlying securities, which is often referred to as a premium or discount. If people get warm fuzzy feelings about the fund manager, there may be more demand, or if not, then less.

Exchange Traded Funds (ETFs) are a bit of a cross-breed between open and closed-end mutual funds. Technically, funds cannot be added to an ETF, so it has a premium or discount associated with it. However, shares can be created by Authorized Participants. APs provide liquidity for an ETF by monitoring the premiums and discounts. If an ETF is selling at a premium, the AP will take the components of an ETF, package them up and create additional shares. If there is a discount, the ETF will buy the shares and then sell the individual components. Either way, the AP makes a profit.

With all three of the major investment vehicles, there are a few items to keep in mind. Each mutual fund or ETF may have different diversification goals. Some may focus on the S&P 500, some are going to have a wider focus. Also, there are many actively managed mutual funds and even some actively managed ETFs, so know what you are getting into before you buy.

Risky Business

One of the dumbest exercises that high schools engage in has to be stock picking competitions. Typically, students in some economics classes are allowed to pick stocks and invest a hypothetical $10,000. The student with the best return after a month or two wins. Basically, we're training kids that making stupid decisions can pay off.

There are a lot of risks inherent to investing. Recognizing those risks is the first step in understanding the concepts behind diversification.

Credit risk mostly affects bonds (which are loans to corporations or governments). It is the possibility of loss due to a company's inability to pay its debts. So if XYZ Corp fails to make an interest or principal payment to bondholders, the value of other bonds is going to fall dramatically. This makes sense. If a company defaults on one obligation, the possibility of defaulting on another seems pretty good. As for the stock price, would you want to buy a company that can't pay its bills? Yeah, neither does anyone else.

Currency risk has a negative impact on your investments as a result of currency movements. However, it doesn't just affect companies with major international operations. It affects all companies that buy or sell internationally, which is pretty much every company in the United States. Obviously, the more enmeshed in international business a company is, the more of a threat currency risk presents.

For the larger international corporations who may have subsidiaries in other countries, their financials can be greatly affected by currency translation. There is an entire topic on currency translation for the CPA exam, which still gives me nightmares.

Currency risk even poses a threat to small companies. The strength of the U.S. dollar waxes and wanes. With a strong dollar, purchasing goods or machinery from foreign companies becomes a boon. Items purchased from foreign companies are denominated in the foreign currency, which is worth less than the dollar. On the other hand, when the dollar is strong, selling to foreign corporations becomes harder because foreign currency doesn't buy as much.

Reinvestment risk is more of a bond problem than a stock problem. The issue that an investor faces is what to do with the cash flows from a bond. When interest rates are declining, the payments received from bonds are not able to be reinvested at the same rate as before. So if ten years ago an investor purchased a bond at 5% per year, they may have to reinvest the payments at the prevailing rate of 3%.

Tired of the old expression that a dollar isn't what it used to be? Well, too bad, because it's true. Inflation risk is here to stay, and it is a completely rational fear to have. If your investments do not keep up with inflation, you are actually losing money as you make money. Many of my clients fall into this trap when they have too much money in their bank account. Wait, too much money in your account can be a bad thing? Let me explain. Cash is the only surefire way to make sure you lose money. The bank is not going to pay accountholders at a pace that will keep up with inflation. Banks are fighting their own battles with reinvestment risk, interest rate risk, and credit risk with their loans, and they are not going to lose money on their deposit accounts. So while cash may feel like the safest investment, it's chock-full of inflation risk.

Concentration risk is probably the most prevalent risk that I see when prospective clients come through my door. It usually goes something like this: Husband or wife has been at ABC Corp for 15 years. Through that time, they have been collecting all sorts of stock. They have participated in the employee stock purchase program, been granted options, have restricted stock units, and may have even purchased company stock in their 401(k) or profit-sharing plan.

Are these people crazy? Yes, they are. They have millions of dollars of their net worth, decades of their life's work, all tied up in a single stock. Not only that, their paycheck is also derived from the same company. It's easy to imagine the scenario in which ABC Corp makes a few bad decisions, their stock price ends up tanking, and then the company decides it needs to produce better earnings per share. What does ABC Corp do? It starts reducing expenses (i.e., laying people off). First on the block are higher-earning employees. So not only has the value of the stock tanked, but the person is also out of a job.

This is not a hypothetical situation. This exact thing happened to thousands of people at Enron during its scandal and ensuing collapse in 2001. Enron had encouraged its employees to invest heavily in the company. In a year, the Enron 401(k) plan lost about $1 billion. A few weeks after the net worth of employees had been decimated, those same employees (almost 21,000 of them) had to start looking for new jobs.

Concentrating investments and putting one's entire net worth in a single company is begging for trouble and grossly negligent. On a risk-adjusted basis, there is virtually no advantage gained through concentrating a portfolio in one stock.

Market risk is the one risk that cannot be diversified away. Quite simply, there are times when the overall markets do well, and there are times when the overall markets do poorly. Sometimes, there is no place to hide. In 2001, when the World Trade Center buildings were destroyed by terrorists, there was a disruption in the markets. There was the physical disruption, in that nothing in New York was open and the stock market did not reopen until September 17.

Then, when the markets did reopen, the Dow dropped 684 points (about 7%). The Deutscher Aktienindex (DAX), located in Germany, reopened on September 12 and dropped 330 points (about 7%). Japan's Nikkei dropped 520 points (about 5%).

This, of course, does not compare with 2008–2009, when the world markets dropped nearly 50% and it looked like civilized humanity had finally met its match. Some advisors thought they saw it coming in the U.S. and moved their clients' money to international markets. Others saw it coming in Europe and moved money to the U.S. Others still moved all their money into bonds, but these advisors were few and far between. Don't think those advisors fared so much better. Many waited too long to get back into the market and ended up losing in the long run.

Constructing a Portfolio Like a Pro

Despite the potential boredom involved, learning about the principles of academic portfolio construction is an important piece of education for millennials. While I don't expect anybody to become an expert in modern portfolio theory or three-factor models after reading this section of the book, my hope is that you will have an understanding of why long-term investing can and should happen, using the outline below.

While Markowitz ignited the fire that reexamined how individuals and institutions should look at portfolios and diversification, it took a great many other minds to add logs to that fire and turn investing into a scientific endeavor. Through decades of research, academia has devised a way to help maximize risk and reward. Remember, there is no such thing as a free lunch, and you cannot be rewarded without taking risk.

When constructing a portfolio, use this three-factor model of known risks worth taking:

1. Market risk

2. Size risk

3. Value risk

Market Risk—What the First Little Piggy Never Told You

Although we covered market risk in the last section, it's important to narrow the definition a bit. Market risk is the ever-present risk that the stock market as a whole can start sucking at any given moment. The stock market is driven by a lot of factors, including world events and the economy. Over time, the market tends to go up faster than bonds.

This is not to say that everybody should have all their money in the stock market. Clearly, holding all of one's net worth in stocks is not appropriate for most people. It's not just an age or time horizon issue. It's also a difference in risk attitude among investors. Every person has a set of perceptions and circumstances. When investors look at their age and net worth, they are only taking circumstances into consideration.

Sacrificing perception of risk and solely basing investment decisions on circumstances yields terrible results. Perceptions are at least as, if not more, important than circumstances. It's relatively easy to change circumstances, and circumstances can be worked around in an investment plan or addressed on the fly as they change; changing perceptions, on the other hand, is like bending steel.

What makes up our perceptions is our personal history and the context under which our history occurred. I can talk until I am blue in the face to someone from the Greatest Generation or Silent Generation (born between 1910 and 1945) about how they shouldn't pay down their mortgage and should just re-stretch their loan in retirement, but I would be wasting my time. That oldest generation doesn't care what the numbers say. They saw the Great Depression up close and personal, and they don't feel secure unless they have a paid-off house.

In economics, there is a concept of risk appetite. The idea is that there are generally three personality types: risk-averse, risk-neutral, and risk-loving. A person's risk personality is what leads them to make any number of decisions ranging from how many heads of lettuce to purchase to whether or not to go bungee jumping. The labels are not judgmental but rather show a preference for a pattern of decisions.

A risk-neutral person weighs the risk and the reward equally. The risk-neutral personality pays attention to risk insofar as the person feels like they are adequately compensated by the reward. Reduction of risk in and of itself provides no benefit for this personality type, but neither does additional risk.

Then there are risk-loving people. These are people who derive joy from taking risk, and not just the outcome. In a Las Vegas casino, risk-loving gamblers would go for the riskiest bets since they derive enjoyment from the risk itself, not just the payout. When risk-loving people invest, they seek out the riskiest investments, not just for the potential payout but also because they want the thrill of the possibility of losing.

A risk-averse person is someone who views risk as an inherently bad thing. This type of person, when faced with a choice, puts heavy emphasis on what the downside could be. When choosing to invest, such a person heavily weighs the potential for loss in comparison to the potential for gain. However, risk aversion stretches along a continuum. Certain people may be more risk-averse than others, making one person's "conservative" portfolio seem very risky to the next. It's all about perception.

The perception of market risk is as important as the risk itself. An investor must be honest with themselves when creating a portfolio that contains market risk. When a risk-averse person takes on substantial market risk, it is a recipe for disaster. That investor has a much higher propensity to sell off during a down market, when that is the worst thing to do. It's better to take on less risk and give up some return but have a portfolio that can ride out the inevitable stormy markets.

Size Risk: It's the Size of the Boat and the Motion of the Ocean

The second part of the three-factor model is size. Size does matter, especially as it relates to investing over long periods of time. When financial people talk about size, they are specifically referring to market capitalization (market cap). The market cap of a stock is determined by multiplying the stock price and the number of outstanding shares. The bigger the number, the bigger the company.

Market cap changes by the minute, and there can be wild swings over short periods of time. Apple, Inc., for instance, had a market cap of almost $750 billion on February 23, 2015, and by May 5, 2015, it had gone down to $726 billion. That's a 3.2% change in a month and a half. While that seems like a drastic drop over a short time frame, Apple trended upward during Steve Jobs's tenure: On August 25, 2011, their market cap was $347 billion.

Sound like Apple is a good investment? Be careful. That type of significant increase is likely not going to happen again for Apple or other similarly sized companies. As it turns out, over long periods of time, small stocks do better than large stocks. Why might this be? When a company is small, doubling earnings, revenue, or any other statistic is much easier. As a company grows, repeating this feat becomes tougher and tougher.

This room to grow lends itself to higher growth over long periods of time. But don't go running to invest in every start-up out there. Higher growth rate comes at a price: risk. Small stocks are generally riskier than large stocks. They're more unstable. They're much more likely to cease operations. They have far less predictability in terms of revenue or any other metric.

Small stocks also have other issues that plague investors. Typically, small stocks don't have a lot of trading volume: There are not as many shares exchanging hands on a particular day. This type of stock is often referred to as thinly traded. Thinly traded stocks can have pricing issues. Large companies have multiple hundreds, thousands, and sometimes hundreds of thousands of people trying to trade, and so the market is well established. There is plenty of supply and demand to get to the true market price. However, small stocks, particularly penny stocks, may only have a handful of people trading them (often called market makers). Even assuming that everybody is on the up and up, it is difficult to discern the true market value of small stocks because there are only a couple of data points. If a market maker is shady, there are multiple ways they can manipulate the system.

Smaller stocks are also often more costly. This often comes in the form of the bid-ask spread, which is the term for the difference between what a market maker is willing to sell the stock for versus what they are willing to buy the stock for. The market maker that facilitates the transactions is paid based upon the bid-ask spread: The wider the bid-ask spread, the more they get paid; the smaller the bid-ask spread, the less the seller gets and the more the buyer pays.

Let's look at an example. XYZ stock is a large company that has high volume; the bid price (what a market maker is willing to pay) is $10 per share while the ask price (what a market maker is willing to accept) is $10.02. The bid-ask spread is $.02. Investor A wants to buy 100 shares; the market maker gladly accepts the investor's $1,002. Around the same time, Investor B wants to sell 100 shares. The market maker then gladly pays the seller's $1,000. What happens to the $2? It is neatly tucked away in the pocket of the market maker.

But a thinly traded stock has a higher bid-ask spread. As a percentage, this number can be quite large. Let's say Company ABC has a bid price of $3 and an ask price of $3.30. The market maker is pulling down 30 cents per share, or 10% of the stock's price. Why is the market maker able to command more of a premium? Simple supply and demand.

When the volume is high, a market maker can have faith that their inventory of a particular stock will move. In other words, there is adequate supply and demand, and they take on little risk that they'll be stuck with the stock. When a stock is thinly traded, they take on the risk they may not be able to procure enough stock to meet future demand or take on risk that demand may not be immediately present.

Small stocks present increased risk both in the performance of the company itself, by means of its management, business model, or quality of product, and by the mechanics of how the markets work. This can make it challenging for the average investor to build well-diversified small-stock portfolios.

Value Risk: Value Stocks Are Not Valuable, and Other Riddles

Value stocks are the third leg of the three-factor stool. A value stock is one that is undervalued, relatively speaking. When evaluating whether a stock is a "value," an investor opens up the company's books and compares the books to the fair market value of the company. The lower the stock price is relative to the books, the more of a value it is. The stock may be undervalued for a variety of reasons. A company could have missed earnings projections resulting in a significant decrease in the stock price. Perhaps there is upheaval in management. Typically, more mature companies are considered value stocks, while up-and-comers are considered growth stocks.

On the other hand, a growth stock is one that is presumably doing really well. When comparing their books to their fair market value, the fair market value is on the high side. From all appearances management seems to be on the ball, earnings are great, and it looks like it's going to be nothing but smooth sailing.

Despite the initial optics, value companies tend to outperform the growth ones. Eugene Fama of the University of Chicago spent a lot of time researching the impact of value stocks, and in 2013 he won a Nobel Prize for his body of work, including his value research. So what did Fama prove?

The key is, while small stocks have room to grow, value stocks have room to surprise. The issue with growth stocks is the expectation. Because their trajectory is so great and they are so well managed, everyone has high expectations for growth. Many investors are willing to pay more for a stock that they think will do really well in the future, and so the price goes up. This price increase is not for the current performance, but expectation of future growth.

Value companies do not have that problem. Nobody really expects them to do anything special. Many times their outlooks are cut, and it shows up as a discount in the stock price. This means that when value companies outperform it is a bigger surprise. This bigger surprise may lead to increased expectations. Because the increased expectations weren't already figured into the price, the price goes up. Of course, there is substantial risk that value companies stay flat or go down.

Understanding the theory of value investing is one thing. Implementing a strategy is quite another. The big question is, how does an investor determine what is undervalued? Investment professionals differ on what it means to be a value stock.

First, some people use the P/E ratio, short for price-to-earnings ratio. The analyst will take the stock's price on the open market and divide by a company's earnings per share and come up with a number. The lower the number, the more value-like the company is. A low number indicates that the price of the stock is low relative to its books. Some will use a forward P/E ratio, where an investor takes the predicted earnings and divides by the price. It's a bit like reading tea leaves, but many think it is a more accurate prediction of where the price is going.

Another method of finding value companies is the book-to-market ratio (BTM). This ratio is comparing the value of the assets on the books to fair market value of the company. If BTM is high, that means the company is more of a value. When the company doesn't have a lot of assets on the books and the fair market value is high, that is an indicator that investors are paying a heavy premium. When there are a lot of assets but the price is low, the premium is smaller, or there is a discount.

Getting Investment Help and Advice—RIAs versus BDs

It's disclosure time. I am a registered investment advisor (RIA). It has never crossed my mind to be anything else because I can't imagine being in a position to place my financial well-being over my client's. If I had my druthers, RIA would be the only option for individual investors. Since I am not king of the world and places like Wells Fargo and JP Morgan Chase have more money than God, making RIAs the only game in town will never happen. In the absence of perfection, I'll take the next best thing: getting the word out about RIAs as much as I can. Now, I am not so jaded as to think that everything about RIAs is perfect or that every RIA is perfect, but in a universe with perverse incentives, the RIA model is usually the best one for the consumer.

A consumer's other advisory option is working with a broker dealer (BD). BDs, such as Wells Fargo, Morgan Stanley, and many others, have broker dealer representatives, usually just called "brokers." Brokers can sell commissionable investment products, whereas RIAs cannot. Brokers are also not held to a fiduciary standard, which means they are not required to put the consumer's interest ahead of their own. They are held to a suitability standard, which means that anything they sell must be suitable for the consumer.

RIAs operate on a fee basis. Many times they collect a fee based upon a percentage of the assets managed, but they can also collect a flat fee. They are paid for their investment advice directly by the client, and not by the product they are recommending—although, in some cases, RIAs can collect commissions on insurance or annuities.

A more interesting trend is the RIA who is dually registered. That is, there are RIAs who are registered with the SEC or state agencies as independent and at the same time registered with BDs and are subject to a different set of standards. Actually, almost two-thirds of

RIAs are dually registered.

What this effectively means is that an advisor can pick and choose whether to apply the fiduciary standard or suitability standard. If a small, unsophisticated investor walks through the door, they can choose to offer a product that has a high commission, even if it isn't in the best interest of the client. Or, when working with a larger client, they can choose to be competitive with other advisors and entice their client to invest more money with a low fee.

The biggest area of concern is that RIAs have a smaller barrier to entry. Basically, take a test, register with the state, and away you go. It may take as little as a month to start meeting with clients, selling, and getting into real trouble. For the most part, though, RIAs do a lot of self-selecting. Some RIAs are castaways from BDs who are tired of working for "the man." Some are talented financial planners sick of referring away good business to investment people. Very few, if any, are bums off the street looking to make a quick buck.

In sum, RIAs are advisors who are required to act in your best interest, and while there can be great variance in philosophies, the end user can be confident when using an advisor in an RIA capacity that their best interests are being considered. The lesson is to watch out for dual registered RIAs—and make sure you are not actually a BD client.

DIY Investing: Preventing Retirement for Generations

I love HGTV primarily because it reminds me that I am not an idiot. My favorite episodes are ones where the homeowner attempts a major renovation and ends up with a house with no walls. Then a professional contractor comes in, finishes the work, and the home looks beautiful. I refuse to do any home improvements on my own aside from painting—and even then, my wife fires me halfway through the job and does it herself.

My job is a lot like the professional contractor who comes in to clean up a mess. Truth be told, I have seen it all. I've had prospective clients come in with 100% cash portfolios. I've had others who were almost exclusively in hedge funds. Only on rare occasions do I see those who have simple, diversified, low-cost investments.

Sometimes these poor investment strategies were cobbled together by other advisors, but more often than not, the biggest culprits are the investors themselves. It's not so much that they are bad investors, but rather that they are choosing bad funds. They are clearly falling victim to their behavior/perception biases that were discussed earlier.

My grandmother bought Qualcomm very early on, much sooner than most, on the advice of a family member. She purchased a swath of stock for around $50 per share before the tech boom, and by the early 2000s the price had gone up to around $800; she rode it to the top. She then rode it all the way back down to the bottom.

We've already gone through the psychology of investing, and my grandmother, like many others, let her emotions get the best of her. She did what most people do: hang onto a handful of stocks and hope that you made good picks.

The rationale that I find most often is that the investor wasn't sure which mutual funds or stocks to pick, so they chose a handful to start with. They did some research, mainly by reading an article in The Wall Street Journal or an investment magazine that listed the best performers for whichever year the investment started, and divided the funds accordingly. Of course, there's my favorite carnival barker, good old Jim Cramer. While I love his business model, I hate his advice. Investing should not require sound effects.

Yet, the DIY investor carries on. A few years after their initial picks, they may add to their portfolio, but a different set of funds will be in vogue. The cycle continues until they are sitting across from me with a smattering of stocks and mutual funds in eight different accounts at six different mutual fund companies. The best-case scenario is that they did not sell anything, but most often they have been trying to ride the hot hand.

Don't get me wrong, DIY investing can work... it just usually doesn't. When you look across the landscape, from 1993 to 2014 the S&P returned 9.22%, and the average stock fund investor made 5.02%. The Barclays Bond Index reported a gain of 5.74% over the same time period, and the average bond investor saw a return of 0.71%. Taking into account that inflation was 2.37%, tstock fund investors

**Average Investors Underperform Major Indices —
Annualized Returns from 1998 to 2017**

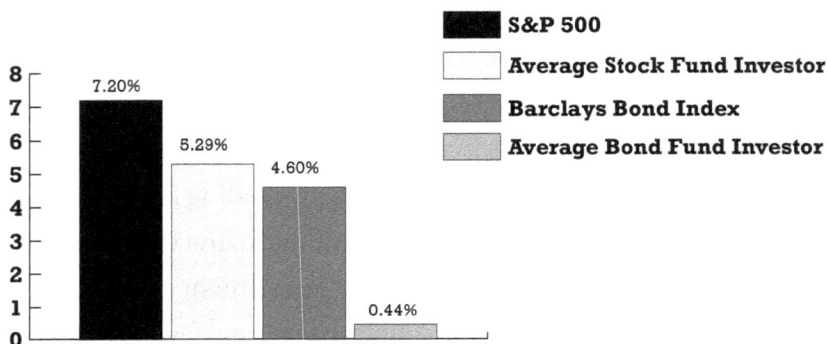

lost half their return to inflation, and the bond investor had a negative return.

This is not particularly shocking. The average investor over that twenty-year period was subject to a roller coaster of emotions. Everything started out rosy, then the tech boom, then the tech bust, then the 2003–2006 run-up, then the implosion, then the recovery. All the while, the DIY investor is dealing with work, kids, saving for college, a mortgage, and their friends bragging about returns. Without the help of an advisor, they are bound to shoot themselves in the foot.

With all this being said, a good DIYer should go for the principles of investing that work:

» Diversification decreases volatility and increases return, as proven by modern portfolio theory.

» Historically, stocks better compensate an investor than bonds.
» Small companies have tended to outperform large companies over long periods of time.
» Value companies have generally outperformed growth companies over the long run.

Finding the right mix between stocks and bonds is a much more difficult exercise for those going it without an advisor. However, it's even more crucial because when times get tough, there won't be an advisor available to talk an investor off the ledge when their finger is on the mouse hovering over the "submit sell" button.

Every prospect I speak to is certain that they can handle market movements, and their tendency is to push for more in the market than their psyches can take. The truth is that I have had prospects choose not to work with me because they felt my recommendations were too conservative. That's okay. My job is to help people stay in their seats when the water gets choppy, and if I think they are taking too much risk and are liable to do damage to themselves, I don't want to help them make a bad decision.

Nevertheless, many investors are hell-bent on doing it themselves and saving the advisor fee. Again, research shows that individual investors are generally better off with advisors, but this book would be pretty bad if I didn't at least give some tips on how someone could construct their own portfolio. Millennials, take out your highlighters.

First, keep your investment principles in mind. Over the last section, I have gone to great lengths to convince you that modern portfolio theory (diversification) is your best option and that there are three driving factors to returns: stocks, small, and value. Stick to your guns.

This is especially true for the passive investor. Because passive investors are fighting their action bias on principle, it's hard to listen to the news (it's a good idea to shut off news relating to investments) or be around friends who are talking about investments. (Is there a mute button for friends who constantly talk about Bitcoin?) Everyone has an idea on what is the next best stock, sector, or mutual fund. Also, for the love of all that is holy, unfollow Cramer on Twitter.

Second, control the controllables. You cannot control the market. You cannot control the Fed. You cannot control the IRS. You cannot control Congress. You cannot control your friends. You cannot control Jim Cramer. You cannot control the gold commercial that constantly plays on the radio.

You can control cost. Cost is an enormous driver of return. The less of a bite the mutual fund company takes out of your apple, the bigger bite you get to take. The average U.S. Large Cap mutual fund has an expense ratio of 1.25%. Keep in mind that actively managed funds often charge a lot more because there is a lot of research being done (despite its futility). ETFs, on the other hand, have an average cost of 0.44%.

You can control diversification. There are thousands of mutual funds in the investment universe. Some funds are only available through advisors, but the average DIY investors still has adequate access to find the mutual fund that suits their needs. There may be people screaming from the mountaintops that you need to invest in a particular fund family, but if that family doesn't fit your diversification goals, then it's not for you.

You can control yourself...hopefully. There will be times when the market is screaming downward and you think to yourself, "Let me sell everything, and I'll get back in when the market is better." This is the most dangerous thought that an investor can have. Once an investor sells, the market is never better enough. There is always some negative news being played because that's what sells the news. By the time cash is reinvested, the market will have likely passed by the point of recovery. Of course, this makes the investor feel worse and can lead to further inaction. Sitting still as the market drops is almost always the best option. When the market goes down, keep in mind that every other investor is in the same boat. They are equally scared. The probability of jumping out of the boat, swimming through shark-infested waters, and making it to a safe, tropical island paradise is slim.

In sum, use an advisor, but if that simply isn't your bag, then find mutual funds that align with your investment ethos. Mutual funds that you end up using, whether with an advisor or not, should be relatively low-cost. In my perfect world, they are not actively traded, and they are well diversified. Apply these same criteria to your IRAs and 401(k)s, if possible.

Check, Please!

When you're at a point where you have real money to invest and are ready to jump into the investment ring, keep the following helpful tips in mind:

1. **A good portfolio is diversified.** Diversification will not save an investor from market risk, but it will buffer against many of the other investing risks that exist. Having pieces of the portfolio that don't correlate perfectly generally leads to higher return and lower volatility.

2. **A good portfolio takes risks worth taking.** Use academia to tell you what kind of portfolio you should have. Over time, small returns are better than large, and value returns are better than growth. Small is riskier than large and value is riskier than growth, and in return investors generally get compensated for that risk.

3. **Though the two look the same, there are important differences between RIAs and BDs.** Every individual RIA and BD will be different, but it's important you do your homework ahead of time. Understand the types of recommendations that each are making before choosing someone to work with.

4. **DIY investing can work, and it's cheaper than using an advisor, but there is a reason why most DIY investors seriously underperform the market.** Temet nosce! Know thyself! It is the most important part of DIY investing. If you are a twitchy investor who sells off positions with the slightest indication of a market dip, paying someone to save you from yourself probably makes sense.

CHAPTER 7

Alternatives: Watch Out for Alternative Facts

They were no match for us. We had this in the bag. There was no way this client was going to go with what this other advisory firm was pitching to them. Alternatives?! LOL. I was just happy I had been invited to this "pitch-off" so that I could see the other guy fail right in front of me.

Our firm had laid out a sane and responsible investment ethos that put a premium on liquidity and transparency. Our solution was to have no alternatives at all, except for adding a liquid real estate fund, which isn't really an alternative investment by anybody's measure.

The other advisor came in with guns blazing. He threw out all kinds of alternative options for the client, publicly traded and non-publicly traded solutions alike—none of which we would ever consider pitching to the client.

As I sat through the other firm's presentation, I had to chuckle to myself. There was no way the client would go for this. I remembered a 2013 study done by University of California-Davis that basically proved how little advantage there is to using alternatives and that most of the success found in alternatives is in very large institutions that can spread adequate capital across multiple hedge funds. And hedge funds are in a space that is fraught with peril. The entire venture is a black box maintained with books that are not kept in Generally Accepted Accounting Principles (GAAP) and cannot be audited. Surely a wise investor would go for the safer bet. This client had an investment board full of smart, shrewd, and skeptical members.

The other advisor got through his presentation, and it was time for Q&A. I couldn't wait to see this guy face the firing squad of questions. I was even starting to feel a bit bad for what he'd walked into.

Little did I know that the client would eat it up. The client thought this advisor had parted the seas and bestowed a gift of wisdom that rivaled King Solomon of ancient Israel. I sat in disbelief. With some of the worst investing ideas that I had ever heard, this guy had won over our customer. A week later my firm was fired from the account, and the assets we were once managing ended up entirely in "alternatives."

I was dumbfounded, but the whole experience did teach me a valuable lesson. Like fashion and music, investing goes through fads and trends as well. The word alternatives held a certain panache for this client. It was outside the box. And who wants to be in the box? I walked away from that meeting knowing how alluring dangerous investment fads can be to an otherwise smart investor.

The category of alternatives include many different flavors, and means different things to different investors and their advisors. When I think of alternatives my mind goes to illiquid assets, basically anything that is not a stock, bond, or mutual fund. There are some alternative strategies that are publicly traded, but they don't fit as neatly into the alternatives box.

Real estate is one popular type of alternative investment. While there are some publicly traded options, the non-publicly traded ones are the riskiest. There are some big commissions for people who sell non-publicly traded REITs (Real Estate Investment Trusts) or who form partnerships to acquire and flip properties.

Annuities are also a type of alternative investment. I know I am in the minority by calling annuities an alternative, but they share some important commonalities with investments that many consider to be an alternative. Annuities are illiquid and can also seem like a black box when you take into consideration their nearly limitless riders.

In this chapter, we'll go through some of the pitfalls that investors may be caught up in when owning real estate, hedge funds, and annuities. We'll review situations in which alternatives might be helpful as well as different elements that should give potential investors pause.

Dishing Out the Dirt on Dirt: Real Estate Investing

I love HGTV. I can't help it. There are so many great shows on the network, my favorite may be about home renovations, but flipping houses is a close second place. There's so much drama, last-minute emergencies, and unrealistic timelines. The before-and-after shots of the homes can at times be breathtaking. It makes for great TV. Real estate investing in general is not always this sexy, though. Flipping houses is one prime example of this type of investment, but there are a few more that, while they may earn you some decent returns, would frankly be terrible TV shows. (Who wants to watch a show about a rental property in the suburbs of Sacramento?)

In addition to flipping houses, real estate investing can include owning residential rental properties as well. Oftentimes, in hot markets like the San Francisco Bay Area, homeowners leave to go to less costly areas of the country and end up renting their former primary residences.

Another type of real estate investment is owning commercial real estate, such as an office building or strip mall. There are also more speculative investments, such as purchasing raw land in undeveloped areas and trying to predict the next city to experience urban sprawl. Investors can also get into hard money lending to contractors looking to finish off a project.

Real Challenges

Maybe it's because I live in Silicon Valley that I see so many people who glamorize real estate investments over other types of investing, even despite what happened to the market in California. From 2007 to 2011, the market crashed hard, even by California standards. Some areas in California were devastated and still haven't recovered from the peaks set in 2006. Yet, many prospective clients that I meet with either have a rental property or are saving towards that goal.

Don't get me wrong. Rental property can make a whole lot of sense, but it is one of those investments where the risk-taker needs to go in with their eyes wide open. Despite the status of being a landlord, it is a lot of hard work. Even when a landlord is working hard, they still may find their property is more of a money pit, and they may have miscalculated the reward for their ownership efforts.

Typically, investors do a back-of-the-envelope calculation when deciding when and how to start owning rental property. They guess at the rent; deduct their mortgage payments, real estate taxes, and maintenance; and then divide by the purchase price to get their rate of return. In California, that number can be anywhere from 3% to 6%. (Notice a management company is not part of the calculation.)

Most people try to live near their rentals so that they can keep a close eye on them and try to avoid paying a management company, which can cost up to 10% of the rental income received off the top. This is the first most likely miscalculation. If a landlord doesn't hire a management firm, that means when the toilet is broken at 2 a.m., the landlord has to get out of bed and take care of it. While there is no monetary cost necessarily, if headaches (like midnight toilet plunges) aren't taken into account, it leads to an overestimation of return. Landlords who choose to go it alone often end up hiring a manager after a year or two, meaning that their initial return calculation needs to be revised and oftentimes is not nearly as attractive as it once seemed.

It's not only the management of home maintenance but also the management of tenants that can make a landlord's life miserable. The level of misery varies by state. In California, where tenants have substantial rights and meaningful remedies against landlords, the cost of doing business is higher. Evicting a bad tenant may take months. In San Francisco, evicting any kind of tenant for almost any reason is virtually impossible. All the while, rent may go unpaid, and there is little that the landlord can do. You can sue for back rent, but good luck getting blood out of that stone.

Another challenge that both novice and veteran rental real estate owners run into is how to calculate true return on investment.

With publicly traded stocks and bonds, there are at least daily valuations and frequent recalculation of yields. This information gets published in newspapers and updated on websites, available anytime to the investor. Real estate doesn't have that. Sales are recorded and published, but because every property is nuanced in some way, the true value is unknown until there is a contract to buy it. Zillow is an interesting substitute, but as any real estate professional will tell you, it is an approximation at best.

This uncertainty poses a challenge, as valuation of property has many important uses. Because property (and rent) fluctuates in value, this means that yield also changes. For instance, if an investor purchased a house in 1980 for $60,000 and was receiving $500 a month for rent, their gross yield would be 10%. If, 30 years later, the value of the house was $1.2 million (not unheard of in Silicon Valley), to get a similar yield, the rent would have to be $10,000 a month.

Property is also subject to a substantial barrier to exit. When looking to sell a property, you have to factor in real estate commission and other costs involved. Typically, that commission plus expenses ends up being around 6% per transaction. Using the previous example, the seller isn't going to net $1.2 million but rather $1,116,000.

Finally, one of the biggest problems with real estate is liquidity. The asset cannot be converted to cash quickly. Even merely taking out a loan on the property to get some additional cash flow may take a month or two. With publicly traded stocks and mutual funds, cash can be available within a few days, and there is a ready market to transact on. The standard closing period on a house is thirty days— and that's after you've found a buyer.

Real-izing the Advantages

Real property does have some amazing advantages, though. Because I am a CPA, the tax advantages are what makes real property so attractive. First, Congress allows for depreciation. Depreciation of residential property is taken straight-line, over 27.5 years. A taxpayer isn't allowed to depreciate land, so the entire cost of the property has to be separated (somewhat arbitrarily) between land and building. If the value of the property is high enough, income can possibly be wiped out. Also, married-filing-jointly taxpayers who make less than $150,000 can deduct up to $25,000 (or a portion, depending on AGI) of loss from rental property against ordinary income.

Long term, it's highly likely you'll be selling the property at a capital gain, meaning you'll be making some money from the sale price. This seems like a good thing, but unfortunately, the tax man giveth and the tax man taketh away. Under Internal Revenue Code (IRC) Section 1250, depreciation is recaptured (taxed as income) when the investor sells. So if thirty years ago an investor purchased a property with a building worth $100,000 and now wants to offload the property, because the building has been fully depreciated, they will have to pay a 25% tax on the first $100,000 of gain and then lower rates for the remainder. Also, some expenses on the property are considered improvements and must be capitalized and depreciated over a period of time. This means that big cash flow items cannot be deducted in the year incurred.

Don't like paying tax when selling an investment property? No problem! The IRC has Section 1031. Under Section 1031, an investor can swap properties tax-free with somebody else. The tax basis is kept, but any cash received or debt relieved is considered taxable income. However, there is no penalty for purchasing a more expensive property or taking out additional loans to buy a better income-producing asset.

Properties also come in a variety of forms. Residential real estate is always top of mind for my clients, but commercial properties are an interesting option for those who want to be more hands-off and have some more stability. Triple net leases (often abbreviated as NNN) make the lessee, not the landlord, responsible for real estate taxes, repairs and maintenance, and insurance. Basically, the lessor's job is to collect checks. The yield won't be as great for the buyer as with residential non-California property, but neither will the headaches.

Despite the romanticism involved with owning real estate, there are some real areas of concern. Whether or not the benefits outweigh the drawbacks is really up to the individual investor. The mantra that we have in my firm is that there are "people who are built for real estate and people who are not." If you are a handy person with a lot of patience, real estate could be a very good asset to hold.

Annuities: The Ice Pick of the Investment World

Annuities are kind of like ice picks. There are few situations in which they are truly useful. According to detective shows, ice picks are primarily used to murder people. I've heard some people actually use ice picks to break up ice on their driveway. But growing up in Illinois, which has its fair share of snow and ice, I never saw an ice pick. So how useful is an ice pick, really? Many of my clients ask this same question about annuities.

An annuity is a tax-deferred vehicle used for retirement income. The investor chooses an investment within the annuity, and the annuity is credited with interest. The investor is not taxed on the growth of the assets as the growth is happening—taxation comes later. If all goes according to plan, in retirement, the investor is paid regular monthly payments. Part of that monthly payment is made up of the very money they put in ("return of capital"), and this portion is not taxed. However, the other part of that monthly payment is made up of gains. These gains are taxed at ordinary rates.

It has been said that annuities are sold, not bought, meaning insurance agents and other financial advisors push hard for clients to purchase them. Indeed, annuity sales typically net bigger commissions for salespeople than other products. Sadly, however, they are inappropriate for the vast majority of people who buy them. So why the appeal?

Annuities can be a good option for old insurance policies with high cash value. A long-term policy may have severe tax consequences if surrendered. It's possible to exchange these policies for an annuity tax-free under IRC Section 1035. So if insurance is no longer needed but there is a large gain built into the surrender value (meaning you'll have to pay a lot in taxes to end the insurance policy), it can be moved over to an annuity to remove the cost of the premium and increase income production.

Annuities can also be good gadget investments. Because of flexibility of the contracts, insurance companies have designed a bunch of riders, some tailored to very particular situations. Most riders are worthless and provide little benefit to investors, but there are some that are quite interesting, like long-term care riders. Many investors can't qualify for a long-term care insurance policy, but annuities can be less discriminatory. Of course, riders cost money, and sometimes they add well over 1% to the cost of an annuity.

Annuities: A Cornucopia of Bad Options

Annuities come in all shapes and sizes, but they can be broken down into three basic types: fixed, indexed, and variable.

All three types of annuities have their own quirks that appeal to different types of investors. All annuities require an owner and an annuitant. The owner is the person paying for the annuity. The annuitant is the person whose life is being measured for the annuity. Often, the annuitant and the owner are the same person, but that isn't always the case. Once the annuitant dies, the contract is over, and the remaining value of the annuity goes to a beneficiary.

Fixed annuities are probably the most useful—and least subject to all the add-ons and expenses that you see in other types of annuities. A fixed annuity looks a lot like a CD. There is a stated rate of interest that does not vary. Like a CD, there is a term of years that the annuity runs (typically between three and seven years). The longer the term, the higher the interest rate. The insurance company that sells the annuity can let the owner pull a certain amount penalty-free every year, but anything above that is subject to penalties, if still in the first few years of ownership. Since annuities are highly customizable, you'll want to check your contract before pulling out any money.

An indexed annuity (also called a fixed indexed annuity or FIA) lets investor put their money into an index fund...sort of. When the money is invested, it sets an anniversary date for the policy. Upon every anniversary, the given index fund is either at a gain or a loss. If the index fund is at a loss, the investor does not participate in the loss. If the index fund is up, the investor participates up to the cap point. The cap point is the upper limit of returns for the investor. Typically, the cap is somewhere between the first 4% to 6% of index return, and the longer the annuity duration, the greater the cap point.

For example, an investor purchases a five-year 5% point-to-point cap for $100,000 with the S&P 500 as the benchmark. In Year 1, the S&P is up 8% year over year. What does the investor make? Remember, there is a 5% cap, so the investor will collect the max of $5,000. What happens to the additional 3% that the money earned? The insurance company keeps it! Year 2, the S&P is down 10%. How much does the investor lose? Nothing! This seems like a good deal. When the market is down, FIAs look great. However, given that the market trends upward 66% of the time, the insurance companies usually come out the winners.

Finally, the most misleading type of annuity: a variable annuity. This type of annuity gives an investor a list of potential mutual fund options, and the investor can choose how to invest their annuity money. The investment list nearly always consists of proprietary funds. Proprietary funds are ones that the insurance company controls and owns. These proprietary funds often have very high internal costs, which, again, add to the expense of the annuity. A variable annuity is mainly a mutual fund type of investment in an annuity shell.

Between the types of annuities and all the riders that can be added, annuities are the ice cream sundae of investment suckage. Though they may look inviting, they're generally awful for you.

Beware of Annuities Dressed in Sheep's Clothing

My ire is aimed not at every annuity, but at variable annuities. Variable annuities, like mutual funds, invest in the market and can have a mix of stocks and bonds. Although these mutual funds look like any other type of fund an investor can purchase on the open market, they cannot be easily looked up and analyzed and are often wrapped in high expense ratios. And the worst part is that greedy annuities salespeople are taking advantage of investors every day.

Consider my friend: He is a successful CPA. He is really smart. He is married to another CPA. She is really smart, too. One day, over lunch, he started telling me about a $100,000 insurance policy he had just picked up. He said some of it would be invested in the market, so I thought he had just bought a variable universal life policy. But then he threw in, "Yeah, and it'll also give me an income stream in retirement." He had just bought an annuity. When I told him this, he laughed. "There's no way," he said, and walked me through the sales pitch. It went a little something like this (I may have made some minor embellishments to prove my point):

Hi, Mr. and Mrs. Millennial! I know you're struggling with nightly intrusion thoughts about what would happen to your two small children in the case of your untimely death. How would they be taken care of financially? Well, boy, do I have an amazing opportunity for you. How would you like to throw a bunch of money at the problem and also save for retirement at the same time?

My company is offering a "life insurance policy" (stifled laughter) that will give you an income stream when you retire. The best part is that the income stream is a guaranteed amount . . . you can't lose money! You'll be able to invest in the stock market, and if the market takes off, you'll benefit.

But what happens if the market goes down like it did in 2008 when you were just getting out of college? Here is some great news: my big insurance company has you covered. For a small annual fee, my company will automatically increase your income stream by a guaranteed amount annually. That's right, when you contribute $100,000, my company will increase your initial investment by 5% every year when calculating the income stream. The market can be down by 50%, but you'll still get your 5% income stream growth. The other good news is that you'll get tax-deferred savings.

Should you die before retirement (pesky intrusion thoughts), your beneficiaries will get a death benefit of $250,000. No matter what, you cannot lose. You'll be covering your children, which is your primary concern, you'll be covering a good portion of your retirement (also important), and you won't be paying me a fee to do any of it.

Let's dissect this horseshit, because while this pseudo-hypothetical salesperson wasn't exactly lying, he wasn't exactly telling the truth either.

The first sin by omission was the cost. The salesman let the couple know that they would be participating in the market should it go up. This is true, but the hurdle to start making money is high.

Annuities, particularly variable annuities, are expensive. I can pretty much end the discussion there, but the world really needs to know just how expensive and how the life insurance companies layer on fees to make sure that the annuity relationship mainly benefits one side (the insurance company). According to the Wall Street Journal, that guaranteed 5% annuity can end up costing investors more than the benefit.

The first expense is the administrative expense. Often, the annuity companies justify this expense as a fee used to pay for the cost of mailing out statements to the customer or interacting with the customer on the phone. As with everything in the annuity universe, this fee has a wide variance. It can range from 0.10% on the low end all the way up to 1.4%.

Next, there is my particular favorite, the mortality expense (usually referred to as M&E). What happens if you die before taking out any payments? Usually your beneficiaries will get the premiums you put in and possibly, depending on the riders you choose, an additional death benefit. What's really happening? The investor is paying the insurance company for a return of premium.

When an insurance company takes on an investor, a certain amount of risk is involved. It costs money to onboard the investor, and to pay out the promised benefits, the insurance company invests the annuity proceeds for the long term. If the investor dies early, there are sunk costs plus possible market risk. To make sure that they don't lose any money in the short term, they charge an annual fee to return premiums. That's right. There is a charge for getting money back that you never even used. It's charming, really. To be fair, the charge is spread among all annuitants so that the people who die early are paid for by the people who die when they are older. I have seen this expense vary, but it can be from 1.25% to 2%.

Also, I would be remiss if I didn't talk about the investment expense ratios. We've already had the discussion about internal cost when it comes to mutual funds (Chapter 6). Well, those same principles apply to the investment vehicles contained inside variable annuities. Often, the investment choices are proprietary funds run by a set of third-party asset managers. Not only do the managers want to get paid, but the insurance company also wants a cut of the investment action. The result is exceptionally high fees for the investments inside the annuity.

In addition, there are riders. Riders are additional features not automatically included in an annuity contract. The sky is the limit with the kinds of riders that can be added to a contract. Some are more popular than others. For instance, there is often an income guarantee rider, such as the one my friend purchased. The initial premium sets a base, and every year the base can go up (for instance, an automatic 5%) or, if the investments did well set a high-water mark from which to draw future payments.

This is how a salesperson can really make some money. Most investors, no matter what level of experience, can sniff out a rat quickly. If all that was offered by an annuity was a shell that held some mutual funds and had a death benefit, no one would ever buy it. However, if you can market it like a retirement planning tool, people will be thrown off track. A rider costs an additional amount;

I usually see 0.5%, but they can be higher. Because a lot of people never invoke riders, the insurance company makes out too.

But what about the guaranteed income stream? It's bunk! First, there was probably a rider attached to it. It's often a guaranteed living benefit, and for a small fee, your living benefit increases by a fixed amount (usually around 5% per year). The problem is the living benefit is not the same as the value of the policy itself. The living benefit only comes into play if you actually start the income stream. However, what usually happens is that income streams are never used. This is where the insurance company makes tons of money. Once you move the annuity or cash it in, you get ZERO value for the income benefit or the associated riders.

Why don't people start the income stream if they paid for it? I've seen a couple of different reasons. First, many find that they don't need the income stream in retirement. Between Social Security and other income sources, they have the money to live and don't want to run up their tax bill with deferred gains from an annuity. Second, and the other side of the coin, many find they need the money as a lump sum. This can be due to medical expenses, or house expenses.

The life insurance is a bad deal too. Often, there is—you guessed it—a small fee for death benefit riders. If you need to protect your family from disaster, grab a cheap term policy (see Chapter 5). Buying an annuity for life insurance purposes is like buying front row seats to a Jerrod Carmichael comedy show merely to see Daniel Tosh. It's just unnecessarily expensive.

Did you notice how the salesperson never mentioned the word "annuity" to my friend? Any semi-experienced professional would know that this is very clearly a variable annuity. There was no point in arguing, though; my friend was locked in for eight years. I dropped the conversation and quickly moved on to other topics accountants and private wealth managers talk about over lunch, like the latest episode of *This Is Us*. But the question continued to bother me: How do two smart, educated people end up investing over $100,000 in a variable annuity? I blame the salesperson and behavioral economics (see Chapter 3). It simply wasn't sold to them as an annuity.

Finally, there are surrender charges. A surrender charge is a penalty for taking out money early. Sometimes there is a free withdrawal of around 10%, meaning that the first 10% you take out has no surrender charge. However, for the majority of the contract, there will be an incentive to keep the annuity in place. Fees on annuity contracts are generally declining. They can be spread out for as little as three years and as many as fifteen years. Most times, I see eight-year surrender periods. Typically, they start at an 8% penalty and drop a percent each year through Year 8.

Here is the tricky part: After eight years, you probably have a tax gain inside of the account. An annuity is tax-deferred, meaning you don't pay tax as you earn money, only when you take it out. Many eight-year periods are "up markets," which means the market has likely gone up, and you will have some gains in your account, despite the high cost of an annuity (although you likely would have larger gains had your money not been tied up inside an annuity for eight years). The gains are not taxed at lower capital gains rates but at ordinary rates, making unwinding them very expensive.

This isn't the case with annuities held inside IRAs. So long as there is a rollover of assets to another IRA account, there will be no taxes due immediately. However, using an annuity inside an IRA is almost always a terrible idea. There is no tax advantage in doing so. Taking away the tax advantage really eviscerates any actual benefit the investor may have with the annuity payments.

So back to the original question: Why do people buy annuities? People love the idea of a guaranteed income stream. They hate the prospect of losing (which is a behavioral bias). The insurance company seems to be offering a good deal. The problem is that it's a good deal for the insurance company. Insurance companies are not in the business of losing money, and they will never set themselves up to lose. Sometimes they make stupid investment decisions that set off worldwide recessions, such as overconcentrating in commercial paper of a particular company (see AIG and Bear Stearns in 2008). For the most part, though, they have annuities down to a science.

If an advisor (insurance, financial, or otherwise) ever tries to talk to you about guaranteed retirement payments, run as fast as you can. As with many things in life, if it sounds too good to be true, it probably is.

Trimming the Hedges

Hedge funds are the James Bond of investing. They are mysterious. They are sexy. They don't follow the rules. And they drink their martinis shaken, not stirred.

Okay, not sure about that last one, but you catch my drift. Hedge funds are largely unregulated so they can invest in whatever they want. If they see an opportunity to buy entire blocks of houses, they buy it. Are man-made snowflakes the future? They'll invest in that. They analyze opportunities and pounce. There are seemingly no limits for hedge funds.

That's why hedge funds always seem to be in the news (usually for the wrong reasons). Typically, higher net worth investors end up in hedge funds, but given their mysterious nature, everyone is at least a little interested. The truth is that hedge funds are a great way to lose money and not even know it. Hedge funds are not subject to the same types of disclosure rules as mutual funds. This means they don't have a prospectus, and they don't have the same reporting requirements. As a matter of fact, there are lots of reasons hedge funds are a bad idea.

» Do you like to know how your money is being invested? Don't buy a hedge fund.
» Do you like to be able to access your money quickly and easily? Don't buy a hedge fund.
» Do you like your investment to be required to report to you current market values? Don't buy a hedge fund.

» Do you like to keep more earnings than your fund manager? Don't buy a hedge fund.

It's obvious that I do not like hedge funds and think they are inappropriate for the average investor—the above reasons are some of the ones that really irk me. The first problem is that a hedge fund is a black box. You truly don't know what exactly is inside because there are few rules to disclose such things. They do have to give a Private Placement Memorandum (PPM), which has some information, but it's mainly a lawyerly exercise of CYA. Look up any Morningstar report on a mutual fund or ETF, and you at least get a glimpse of what your investments are doing.

All a hedge fund investor really knows is that money gets sent to the hedge fund, perhaps there is some reporting, and then money comes out in terms of dividends or other types of income. This is part of what makes the tax reporting on hedge funds so ridiculous. Having worked for Deloitte Tax, I got to see some crazy K-1s, which report the hedge fund earnings for tax purposes. When I saw my first 20-page K-1, I couldn't figure out what such an investment was doing. As it turns out, nobody else can either.

The other aspect of hedge funds that I take umbrage with is the lack of liquidity. Sometimes the fund has a lock-up period, which means that for a period of time the investor is simply not allowed to take money out. Even when there is not a lock-up period, hedge funds are free to limit redemptions to periodic distributions so that cash can be taken out monthly or perhaps even less frequently.

To make matters even worse, hedge funds may also have the right to suspend redemptions. Meaning that if the investor needs their money in a downturn, that investor may be unable to tap into hedge fund investments. Even when you can take your money out, there still may be a sizeable withdrawal fee for the privilege of doing so.

Truth be told, being completely in the dark about your investments and unable to get your money out easily would be forgivable sins if the returns made up for it. The problem is that nobody knows if the returns make up for it. Nobody really knows what hedge funds' collective returns are. Because hedge funds are not required to maintain a consistent methodology, most of the time investors have no idea what they are getting themselves into.

That's right—reporting for benchmarking is completely voluntary. There are databases that collect the returns of hedge funds, but a hedge fund is free to participate or not participate in such databases. They can also choose to start and stop reporting at any time. There are lots of reasons to stop reporting performance. Perhaps the hedge fund no longer needs subscribers because it is so successful. Or perhaps the hedge fund is embarrassed by losses. This is often referred to as self-reporting bias.

Hedge fund investing opens up a whole new world of biases for investors to consider. Smoothing bias occurs because many hedge funds own assets that are not liquid or marketable, such as real estate or businesses. When the hedge funds report, they must value these illiquid assets, and conveniently for hedge funds, they report very little change in the valuations of illiquid assets. This is highly unlikely to be the truth. In the case of real estate, we know that real estate is just as variable as any other asset class, so we would expect wild swings up or down.

Like mutual funds, hedge funds also suffer from survivorship bias. The truth of the matter is that about 15% of hedge funds disappear each year, and the average hedge fund lasts only five years, as reported by Hedge Fund News. According to CBS News, survivorship bias may skew the returns of hedge funds by up to 4.4%. When paired with self-reporting bias, using performance data is laughable.

Backfill bias is a problem that occurs within hedge fund indices. When a manager wants to include their fund in an index, they typically must provide at least 12 months of data. The problem is they can choose which data and which time periods to include. So if they have five funds and only one has done well, they can choose to omit the last four. Has the fund had a really bad start but a great last couple months? Fund managers can select to report on just the last year. Any research done on hedge funds (especially small ones) is at best irrelevant and at worst delusional.

As horrible as investments with hedge funds are, the coup de grace is the cost. How much does one need to pay for an investment that has unreportable performance, poor liquidity, and an incomprehensible amount of complexity? A lot. The typical hedge fund takes a 2% management fee right off the top. That isn't so bad. After all, a fee-based mutual fund money manager usually takes somewhere around

1%, and what is an extra 1% annual compounded rate of return among friends?

It gets worse. Most hedge funds operate on the two and twenty compensation system. Not only do they get their guaranteed 2%, but when an asset is sold at a profit, they take 20% of the gain of the asset right off the top.

Let's look at an example. You put $1,000,000 into a hedge fund. After Year 1, your hedge fund's assets are valued at $900,000. Good news: you only owe your hedge fund manager $18,000 (which is 2% of $900,000). Let's say the next year is a good one and the hedge fund sells its interest in an Arizona snow plow company for a $100,000 profit, and there are other investments in the account, and it goes up to $1,100,000. First, you'll pay your hedge fund manager $22,000 (which is 2% of $1,100,000), and then you'll pay him another $20,000 via the 20% success fee. This will leave you with $1,058,000. Your 10% rate of return based on initial investment has gone down to 5.8%.

It gets even worse. Some hedge funds are a "fund of funds." What this means is the hedge fund manager is so smart that he or she can tell which other hedge funds are good and which ones are bad and chooses a portfolio of the good ones. Not only does the underlying hedge fund manager get 2% and 20%, but so does the manager of the fund of funds.

If I still haven't convinced you that hedge funds are the biggest joke in the investment universe, or perhaps the actual universe, read this: According to Bloomberg, from 2009 through 2013, hedge fund returns trailed the S&P 500 every single year, and as of the end of 2013, still had not made the recovery back to their 2007 highs. And this is just the information from hedge funds that were willing to report. Can you imagine what the actual performance would be if all hedge funds would have dutifully reported? The Bloomberg Hedge Funds Aggregate Index tracks over 2,200 funds, of which less than 60% reported in December 2013. Maybe they didn't report because their returns were so spectacular that they didn't want to embarrass the poorer performing hedge funds.

The good news is that hedge funds have to go after accredited investors. Generally, these are institutions including banks and pension plans, as well as charities, partnerships, and trusts with $5 million or more in assets. Also included are individuals with net worth in excess of $1 million, or married couples with more than $300,000 of annual income, or individuals with more than $200,000 of annual income. So, really, it's the one percenters that have to look out. That being said, many teachers may want to check in with their pension plans to see how much is allocated to hedge funds.

Check, Please!

If you're the type of person who really likes to be "outside the box," you may be drawn to alternative types of investing. If so, be sure to go into it with eyes wide open and keep the following tips in mind:

1. **Real estate is an alluring investment.** There are some

great benefits that can come along with it. Deferred gains on capital appreciation combined with depreciation that can shield current income are compelling reasons to look at real estate.

2. **Not all real estate investments are created equal.** Be careful of what type of real estate investment you choose. Rental real estate is very hands-on. Investing in real estate partnerships puts you at the mercy of a managing group. Mutual funds have internal costs. Liquidity should always be top of mind when choosing real estate.

3. **Annuities can be useful tools when used properly.** They offer some tax benefit and are an option for some types of life insurance policies. They are contracts, so they come in limitless varieties of suck.

4. **Watch out for annuity costs.** The flexibility and riders cost money and can take a serious bite out of your return. The cost of annuities often are not readily available, and you'll have to break out the investment prospectus to get the full picture. Remember, if you want to get out of an annuity, you may have to pay an additional surrender charge that may go as far out as eight years.

5. **Just say no to hedge funds.** Nancy Reagan's war on drugs was idiotic, but my war on hedge funds is completely justified. While they may look sexy, hedge funds make a lot of money for their managers but have very little value to investors. To top it off, hedge funds are illiquid and mind-bogglingly complex.

CHAPTER 8

Financial Vampires: Twilight Gone Wrong

If you work for one of the fewer than 50 companies that will go public or have a buyout this year, congratulations! Working for a company through this transition is, at worst, a unique experience and, at best, a lucrative time for employees. As you can probably imagine, predatory advisors know you have more money sitting in your bank account and will find your contact info to spam you with offers for real estate deals, investment deals, annuities, and other more exotic "opportunities." I had a client who had no less than fourteen voicemails from advisors looking to set up a meeting—the day the deal was announced.

In fact, this can happen to any working person of a certain age because advisors know that, over time, a working person will typically have more cushion from paycheck to paycheck and more money to consider investing. Additionally, the Internet tracks our movements and sells our information to others so that they can then try to sell us some product or service based upon our browsing and purchasing history.

As Biggie said, "Mo' money, mo' problems." Investors experience additional frustration when having to pick through the mountains of options for what to do with their money. Analysis paralysis sets in, and all advisors start to look the same. But not all advisors are the same, and understanding their motivations and how they all fit in with your goals is critical to finding the correct solutions. Before an investor can consider solutions, they need to understand the nature of the data they will be looking at.

In this chapter, we'll dive into what Wall Street says you should be interested in. We'll discuss the dangers of actively managed funds, the difference between advisors and important considerations when choosing someone to work with. Finally, we dive deeper into the dark side of annuities and insurance.

Dirty Secrets of Active Fund Managers

Active management is a multibillion-dollar industry. There is a reason for this. Mainstream investors all want to believe they can find someone to beat the market by trading tactically. They hire advisors, mostly MBAs and fund managers, and pay them a percentage of their investment to actively manage their money. But the numbers show this is a losing proposition. You may be asking, "If active management is such a losing strategy, how do the managers stay in business?" Easy—they fudge the truth. Notice I didn't say lie because I want to avoid being sued. There are perfectly legal ways to shade the truth.

The primary way that managers attempt to make their portfolios better performers is by using their discretion to purchase securities that will be winners. Every fund has a stated purpose. For instance, they can be dedicated to choosing stocks in the small cap international space or picking stocks in the S&P 500. However, if you read the prospectus closely, it almost always leaves the door open to other investments, usually by stipulating that the fund manager can select other assets her or she may deem appropriate.

This can be misleading to investors because they are expecting to be invested in a particular way, but in reality they can be in something completely different. Imagine going into a cupcake shop, asking for an assortment, and being handed a box of cookies. Worse yet, imagine you were handed a case of kale. The kale scenario more or less happened in 2013 when a mutual fund that was supposed to be in the stock market ended up being 65% invested in cash!

Another way that mutual fund companies try to obscure results is by using survivor bias to their advantage. A fund family only has to report the funds that are currently operating; thus, when a mutual fund fails or has a bad stretch, the mutual fund company will either merge the fund with a better performing fund or just kill off the fund and let the investors reallocate. This means there's no true way to ever know how the fund family is performing or has performed in the past.

What is even more insidious is when mutual fund companies incubate a fund. Fund incubation is when a company chooses several managers to start several funds at the same time. Each fund is allowed to operate for a number of years somewhat under the radar. After the term of years is up, the company takes the best performing fund and makes it a star on their offerings platform. The other funds are merged or disappear and are never mentioned again.

Similarly, this is how companies get to advertise on television commercials that all of their funds beat the respected averages or benchmarks. They simply nix all of the funds that weren't successful and therefore do not have to mention the failed funds to prospective investors.

As you can imagine, the biggest problem for active funds is consistency. Remember that consistency among fund managers is a fallacy with only 2.1% of top quarter mutual funds remaining in the top quarter after five years. When only the top performers are allowed to survive, there is seemingly no way for managers to sustain that level of success because nearly all funds eventually return to the mean. The people left holding the bag are the consumers. They had been told that entire fund families beat their averages, only to have their fund be part of 97.9% of mutual funds that cannot repeat their performance over the following five years.

Despite everything I have just outlined, active management still predominates the landscape—by a lot. Only 38% of money in mutual funds are passively managed. That's up from 3% in the early 1990s. People certainly seem to be getting wiser, but the majority of investors still seem to be holding on to hope that they are going to pick the advisor who can pick the manager who can consistently pick the stocks that will beat the market, despite the odds and history to prove otherwise.

The best way you can ensure that you are in passive funds is just by doing a little bit of research. Every publically traded mutual fund produces a turnover ratio. The turnover ratio tells investors how many of the holdings change over a year as a percentage. So, generally speaking, if a fund has a 100% turnover ratio, that means by the end of the year an investor can expect the portfolio to be completely different. The higher the ratio, the more active the fund. You can find the turnover ratio of a fund many places, but Morningstar.com is a good place to start.

Understanding Who Has Your Best Interests at Heart—And Who Does Not

Investing used to be easier. Not necessarily better, just easier. If you wanted to invest in the stock market, you used a broker. Done. That was a very easy process. There were commissions involved, but because it was virtually the only game in town, why worry about cost?

Oddly enough, insurance companies then got in the mix. It used to be that insurance companies just did insurance. If you look at the old State Farm insurance logo, it says "Auto, Fire, Life." If the logo was changed to reflect today's offerings, it would probably say "Variable Life, Mutual Funds, Annuities." Insurance agents can sell a great many investment products—and take every opportunity to cross-sell.

Do-It-Yourself (DIY) investing has become more popular through the years. I believe the greatest reason for the rise in those going it alone is the media. Remember the ad campaign with the E-Trade baby? That kid's a freaking genius. He goes on his iPad and makes loads of cash. The marketing department at E-Trade is the bigger genius. They have people convinced that with the right tools, they can beat the market. Who wouldn't want that? With the rise of robo-advisors, investors are gaining confidence that they don't need an advisor.

The Brakes of Brokers

When the everyday person thinks about an investment advisor, it's usually the stereotypical broker that pops into their head. I think of the movie The Pursuit of Happyness, where a down-on-his-luck medical device salesman (and single father) ends up working at Morgan Stanley. I see a bunch of Will Smith characters huddled in a phone bank dialing numbers as fast as they can. Quick-talking, quick-dealing salesmen trying to get their next fix. One or two make it while the rest die trying.

Most of what we see in the movies is not exactly true, but it's not exactly false either. The broker's life is not an easy one, especially in the beginning. It is hyper-competitive, and most do not make it past their first or second year in the business. There is a large focus on being able to sell products, and many brokers get paid a very small base salary and must rely upon their ability to sell and retain commissions.

What complicates the discussion even more is that brokers are not subject to any fiduciary responsibility to their clients. As a matter of fact, it is legally impossible. Even if an investor loves a broker but wants someone to guarantee in writing that their advisor will work only in the best interests of the client, the broker's compliance department would never let that happen. There are many brokers who do keep their clients' best interests at heart, but the truth of the matter is that brokers do not work for their clients.

The people we typically call brokers are really not. They are actually broker dealer representatives (BD reps). Because everybody in the world knows them as brokers, I'll keep with the vernacular. Brokers act as agents for larger parent organizations called broker dealers (BDs). They must abide by the broker dealer rules, and they are subject to regulatory review from the organization's compliance department.

The name "broker dealer" is a term of art. BDs are investment firms registered with the Financial Industry Regulatory Authority (FINRA). FINRA is a not-for-profit organization authorized by Congress to enforce rules for the BDs. In terms of what a BD is authorized to sell an investor, FINRA has Rule 2111, which states that the firm must have reasonable basis to believe that an investment recommended is suitable for the customer.

You can find a laundry list of criteria on the FINRA website (www.finra.org) for determining the investor's profile and what is suitable, including:

» Age
» Other investments
» Financial situation and needs, which might include questions about annual income and liquid net worth
» Tax status, such as marginal tax rate
» Investment objectives, which might include generating income, funding retirement, buying a home, preserving wealth, or market speculation
» Investment experience
» Investment time horizon, such as the expected time available to achieve a particular financial goal
» Liquidity needs, which is the customer's need to convert investments to cash without incurring significant loss in value
» Risk tolerance, which is a customer's willingness to risk losing some or all of the original investment in exchange for greater potential returns

So long as this guidance is followed and the correct inquiries are made, the broker has very little to worry about in terms of compliance with the law.

But what's best for the client? That question is unimportant. Client A meets all the requirements to invest in both Fund X and Fund Y. Both funds are nearly the same in every respect, except that Fund X is less expensive and has a 3% commission that goes to the broker, and Fund Y is more expensive and has a 5% commission. Which fund can the broker recommend? The answer is either one.

Once a broker has gone through the rubric of suitability, they are off the legal hook, aside from fraud. Because both items are suitable for the client, the broker is free to recommend whichever one he wants. Let's not kid ourselves. If a broker (or any other rational human) had the choice outlined above, how could they not take the one that gives them more commission? While altruism is a worthy goal, if I found out that my broker chose to take less, I'd fire them for being stupid.

But brokers are not stupid. As a matter of fact, they go through hell to get a shot at being successful. They start out in large classes (remember again The Pursuit of Happyness), where it is as cutthroat as it gets. They learn, receive training, and sell, and after a couple of years the cream rises to the top, and you have some very quality brokers. Of course, along the way, the weaker brokers are dropping off, but they are still making sales to trusting customers.

Compensation arrangements are also important to understand. A broker typically gets paid on commission. The commission is determined by the security that is sold. Sometimes there is a load, which is a sales charge. The load can be in the front (meaning taken off the top) or in the back (taken at the end, if holding requirements are not met). There are also 12b-1 fees, which are fees for marketing and distributions. They are sometimes used in part to pay ongoing commission to the salesperson (called a trail), or they are used to defray advertising cost. It's possible, if not likely, for a fund to have both a load and a 12b-1 fee.

I'm not trying to cast aspersions on brokers. There are a lot of brokers who are very competent and forthright. But no matter how scrupulous, there are inherent perverse incentives set up in the system. Also, while the ones who make it out of the process are fairly high quality, the ones who are just starting out may or may not be the best, and they are on the edge of being employed, making an investor's experience choppy.

Insurance Agents (Really)

(Apologies in advance to my friends who are insurance agents...)

An insurance agent selling mutual funds is like an actor performing neurosurgery. It's not that actors aren't smart enough to be neurosurgeons; it's that they have just dedicated their life's work to art, which is not neurosurgery. I love movies, but if I'm on the table for brain surgery and Daniel Day Lewis walks in the room, I'm clutching my gown and bolting.

As any of my clients would confirm, I believe that insurance is an integral part of financial planning. I have millions of dollars of insurance that covers my life, my wife's life, our personal possessions, and our personal liability. But I would never give a shiny red cent to an insurance agent to invest. Insurance agents (and insurance brokers) have dedicated their lives to insurance.

Why would this even come up in conversation? Most insurance brokers that I know (not captive to any particular company), have no inclination to sell anything but insurance. But the captive agents (think Allstate and Farmers) are required by their company to sell a certain amount of investments—something on which they have limited training and can really hurt clients in the long term.

When they are selling mutual funds, they technically work for two parent companies: the actual insurance agency and another separate entity, which is technically a BD (making the insurance agent a BD representative). In the previous section, you learned that BD representatives are held to a suitability standard and are not fiduciaries. By definition, they are not required to act in your best interest. I'm not saying your insurance agent is trying to screw you over, but it is important to know that when making these sales, they are not compelled to put your interests first.

I have been approached by a State Farm agent on a number of occasions to put money into the insurance company's 529 plan, IRA, or start a 401(k). Typically, I leave the office laughing, but there are a number of people who buy the product. I know of one agent who lamented to me that she managed a client's $1 million 401(k) because she had no idea how to advise it. However, her commissions were fantastic.

Millennials are a hot target and are being solicited by insurance companies every day. It's important to know the background before getting inundated with new terms and details. The main point here is that buying insurance from an insurance agent is good but buying mutual funds from an insurance agent is bad. The primary reason is lack of training. I cannot speak for all insurance companies, but I was a captive agent for a few months with a large national insurance company. I received some great training on insurance products, planning around insurance, and general insurance education. I received no training on financial planning. Investments were just another item to cross-sell.

My advice is to strongly decline investment opportunities from your insurance agent—and also neurosurgery from opera singers.

The Dark(er) Side of Annuities

We've already discussed some of the issues with annuities and life insurance (see Chapter 6), but this is where I am really going to tee off. Aside from the couple of fringe scenarios where annuities and permanent life insurance are appropriate, these things don't make sense for the majority of people. Insurance agents bill them as some great investment vehicle. They are not.

What the investor ends up getting is a huge investment hurdle. If they invest with a company on the high end for both mortality, expense fees, and internal cost, they could be looking at upwards of 3.5% per year that goes to the insurance company right off the top. As an investor, this is a terrible proposition. If the market is up 7%, which is not a bad year, you're up 3.5%. You've lost half of your gains!

Let's use numbers to demonstrate how terrible this truly is. Let's say an investor has $1 million. If it were possible to invest in the S&P 500 directly with no costs, which it is not, and the S&P earns 7% per year, at the end of twenty years, the investor would have a bit over $3.8 million. Thank you, compounding interest!

What if you invested in an ETF that had an internal cost of 0.1%? After twenty years, you'd have a little under $3.8 million. If you worked with an advisor and paid them a flat 1% in addition to the 0.1%, you'd have a little over $3.1 million. If we apply a 3.5% haircut from a relatively expensive annuity, the investor would have a little under $2 million. You don't have to be a "math person" to see that this is the worst deal.

I believe in spending money to make money, so what do you get for those high fees? It seems mainly tax-deferred growth. I don't care what tax bracket you are in, you aren't going to save enough in taxes to make up for what is lost to an annuity. You would not make up the $1.1 million difference between using a reasonable fee-based advisor and the high-cost annuity.

While your gains would be tax-deferred, as you pulled out those distributions you would pay income tax at ordinary rates (the same rates that you pay for your W-2 income). While you would have paid taxes on dividends along the way on a non-annuity account, those dividends would be tax-preferred, and the underlying assets would get capital gain treatment. Furthermore, when you die, your beneficiaries get taxed on all the remaining annuity income, while non-annuity accounts get stepped up in basis, and the gains go away.

To be fair, a 3.5% M&E charge combined with internal cost is on the high end. However, there are other costs layered onto an annuity that can easily push it into the 3.5% per-year range. Many insurance agents will push riders hard. As discussed in Chapter 7, a rider is an additional benefit that an investor can purchase from the insurance company. The types of riders vary along with the costs associated with the riders.

Let's use the previously discussed guaranteed income rider. It varies in terms of cost, but I've seen 0.5% most often. The problem with the guaranteed income rider is that most people don't really understand it. The insurance company is essentially saying that no matter what happens in the market, the income stream that you are entitled to receive when you turn it on will go up by a certain amount every year until you turn it off. If the value of your account goes down, it doesn't matter. The income stream (when you turn it on) will be guaranteed not to go down.

So if you invest the hypothetical $1 million that starts off with $60,000 of income at retirement and have a 5% guaranteed income rider, the base for income purposes will grow by 5% a year. This means that in twenty years your income benefit will be around $159,000 per year. However, if you surrender or exchange the annuity, the benefit does not come with you. It evaporates, and you're left with the surrender value, which may not have grown so nicely, given the expense of the product.

This is the essence of the rider problem; it does not increase the surrender value.

The guaranteed income rider guarantees your return for distribution purposes only. It only takes effect when you annuitize. Annuitizing is turning on income for the rest of your life and not being able to reverse the decision. A lot of people choose not to annuitize because they may not need the money when they reach retirement or they don't like the rate of return. The insurance company banks on the fact that people will not use the annuity for the purposes intended. Indeed, around 2.2% of policies are annuitized according to a 2017 Ruark study.

Why You Should Ignore Your Insurance Agent When You Hear the Words "Permanent Insurance"

A large part of what I do involves me selling my services. As a result, I am genuinely understanding when a salesperson is pitching me, whether it be on the phone or in person. I have a rule for salespeople: I will be kind and respectful when listening, but once I say no, the conversation is over. If the salesperson does not respect my decision, then it's game on for me to tear them apart.

My former State Farm agent learned this lesson the hard way. He set a meeting one day for me to come in and review my policies, which is always a good idea. Although I am an insurance agent, I don't do it full-time, so to talk about it with someone who does is a worthwhile exercise.

We sat down and started going over my current coverages. We talked about the insurance per square foot of my home and decided to increase it. My auto coverage and umbrella were fine. He then asked about life insurance. I told him that I have quite a bit of coverage, enough to cover my mortgage, my kids' education, and my wife's living expenses for some time. Then he pitches me on whole life insurance.

I kindly informed him that I prefer term insurance, that permanent insurance is unnecessary, and that I was not interested. It was then that he made his fatal error: "Permanent insurance is a good investment vehicle." I immediately became irritated because 1) he had violated my "no means no" rule and 2) he said something patently ridiculous to a person who makes their entire living actually selling good investment vehicles.

For the next fifteen minutes, I proceeded to tell him how flawed his argument was; how he could keep his 4% return on a whole life policy when, over a twenty-year period of time, the market has a very good possibility of returning much more than that; how even with deferred tax compounding, the numbers still do not add up; and how when I wanted to surrender the policy, I would have a bunch of ordinary income to pay Federal and state income tax on. He waved the white flag.

Variable annuities and variable permanent insurance do have a lot in common when it comes to the benefits and drawbacks. Both offer tax-deferred growth. Both involve expensive proprietary funds. Both have expensive riders that rarely make sense. Both are largely misunderstood by consumers.

What bothers me most about permanent insurance is the possibility that it is horribly mismanaged. Consumers can take loans against the cash value of the insurance policy and are only on the hook to pay themselves back, which sounds fantastic. However, if done incorrectly, the consumers who may truly need the protection of the insurance in case of a catastrophic event may find their policy lapsed, or the loan has eaten away at a large chunk of the benefit. As knowledgeable professionals, insurance agents sometimes need to protect consumers from themselves and not offer these types of policies.

Furthermore, a policy that collapses is still subject to tax. Although a loan taken from a policy is not taxed, once the policy lapses the loan becomes a distribution. The distribution will likely be at least partially taxable. As previously mentioned, when that taxable income occurs, it will be taxed at ordinary income rates. This puts a consumer, who was already in need of financial help, in dire financial straits.

Check, Please!

Feeling a little paranoid that everyone is out to get you and your money? I wouldn't go that far, but you definitely do need to be on guard and make sure that people who want to pitch their products and services really do have your best interests at heart. Here are a few takeaways to help you keep your money out of the wrong hands:

1. **Active investing is a losing proposition.** Although some managers seemingly do better over time than others, it is a complete crapshoot. The probability that an investor can pick the person who can pick the right ponies is very low. Additionally, active investing is expensive and has almost no benefit to anyone.

2. **Choose your advisor wisely.** Brokers are not bad people who have bad intentions, but they do have perverse incentives for recommending various products. An RIA is required by law to be

a fiduciary and make investment decisions in the best interest of the client.

3. **Annuities are expensive and present a large hurdle to achieve investment success.** Salespeople will often try to tack on riders that increase the costs further but which may have little benefit for the investor. Investors need to read the prospectus and understand the details of all of the proposed riders.

4. **Permanent life insurance should really only be used in very specialized situations.** It's not a great investment or savings vehicle. When using the lending part of an insurance policy, it's important that the worst-case scenario be modeled so that the policy does not lapse. A lapsing policy can have serious adverse tax consequences.

CHAPTER 9

Downsizing: When You Love Your Grandkids But Don't Want Them to Visit Too Often

Life is short. For those of us who were born in the early 1980s and have families of our own with houses in the suburbs, the next stop is becoming an empty nester and transitioning to a smaller house. This next stop will also be the time to begin seriously visualizing retirement. Many of our parents are going through this process right now. The younger boomers are on the precipice of retirement, and as they have accumulated along the way, we get to observe what a lifetime of purchasing nets us.

There is a strong lesson to be learned here. As my in-laws and parents start to go through their possessions and make decisions about what stays and goes, I have noticed a curious trend. The possessions that are most valued are differentiated by their representation of experiences versus that of pure consumerism.

The lamp that was the must-have 10 or 20 years ago or the beautiful leather couches are not given much thought. The items they consider indispensable are often souvenirs from trips or artwork purchased during a festival. When we are younger, we tend to think things will make us happier. For a 5-year-old it's the newest toy, for a 16-year-old it's a newer car, and for a 30-year-old it's a bigger house, but along the way we learn that the increased utility is fleeting.

Thankfully, we gain perspective over time. We begin to acknowledge that all the things collected don't hold a candle to the experiences that we have had or will have. At the end of the day, it's just stuff, and the lazy, contrived saying of "You can't take it with you" holds true. What we do take to the grave are our memories.

In law school, the summer after your second year (2L) is spent doing an internship. In my 2L summer, I split my time between the Department of the Air Force and the Sales and Use Tax department at Deloitte Tax. While the Air Force internship was spent in the hole known as Marysville, California, I spent my time at Deloitte in downtown Chicago.

As previously mentioned, I grew up in the Chicagoland area. All of my family is still there, and when I was in law school, three out of my four grandparents were still alive. In fact, my Papa Leon still worked (well into his mid-70s) as a jeweler in downtown Chicago.

My Papa Leon was born in Poland in the early 1930s. He immigrated to Buenos Aires, Argentina, just before the Nazis took over his town. When he was old enough, he joined his family's jewelry business. The family made it through Peronistas, but when the stability of the country was threatened, most of the family made its way to Chicago, including my grandfather, grandmother, father, and eldest aunt.

My grandfather started over again in Chicago living in a small apartment with three kids (my other aunt was born after arriving in America). When I look back on his life, I can say definitively that he lived the American dream. He owned a house in the suburbs, sent three kids to college, and lived independently until the day he died.

While I worked at Deloitte and he worked a few blocks away, we got to have lunch a couple of times. We sat and ate Cajun food and talked about life. It is my fondest memory of my grandfather. All the cool clothes I bought while in the city, the nice lunches with partners that I attended, and the bars I frequented during that summer simply fade to the background. The three or four hours I shared with Papa Leon—that was the most important part.

Despite letting go of our things and letting experiences guide our spending more, we still need to find a way to pay for it. The truth is that more people are working later and later in life or choosing to work part-time while letting their assets supplement their lifestyle. Either way, retirement needs to be planned for, and thankfully, there is an entire industry dedicated to financial planning.

This chapter isn't about downsizing per se. Rather, we're going to explore some common financial concerns that go along with that phase of life, such as what is a prudent level of income to take from a portfolio. We'll also revisit long-term care. Finally, we'll dive into some strategies that can make a seemingly impossible retirement possible.

70 Is the New 50

Retirees are squirrely. I remember the days where you knew exactly where you could find a retiree...at home or in the nursing home. There was never any question of where you could find my mom's father. He was in bed watching either the Cubs game or the stock market. This wasn't the healthiest way to live, but it made for some certainty.

Today's retirees are different. As I mentioned before, many are actually showing up for a job. Perhaps not first careers and perhaps not even paying gigs, but the modern septuagenarian is not sitting idly by while death catches up. This trend will likely continue. The Greatest Generation was one of the first to have a lot of downtime in retirement. They were in better health in retirement and could actually do things like travel or enjoy other hobbies that can cost a lot of money. Prior to that generation, people died a lot younger, so retirement was brief, and health uncertain.

It used to be retirement was maybe 10 years, and that was probably on the longer side. Most worked until they couldn't. Saving for a luxurious retirement was a ridiculous notion. You farmed or worked your factory job, paid off your house, and hoped your ten children would help care for you in your old age. Old age was about age 60 or 65. Imagine the surprise of the greatest generation when they had 15-year retirements to contend with.

I'm actually starting to plan out 30-year retirements for my clients. For the Greatest Generation, 70 became the new 60. They established a new norm. Now, for Boomers, 70 is seemingly the new 50. My guess is that the same trend will hold true for millennials.

From a retirement standpoint, this means that our retirement will be a lot longer than it was for our parents. Millennials may be facing a 40-year retirement, and some even a 50-year retirement. More problematic than that, however, is that a millennial's health should be so much better than in prior generations. This means we'll be able to go to Disneyland well into our 80s with our great-grandchildren, and far from being in a wheelchair, you'll find us on Space Mountain. Taking a cruise in our early 90s won't be that big of a deal.

This is problematic because humans tend to like to live their lives, which requires money. When a retiree has a 20-year retirement, of which the first 10 years are in good health, the money should last. A 40-year retirement with 30 years or more of good health is a different story. The Baby Boomers were lucky enough to inherit a lot of money from their parents in the Greatest Generation. I worry that Gen X'ers and millennials won't inherit nearly as much since the Boomers are going to live longer with a better quality of life.

4 Percent Rules! Or Does It . . .?

Conventional wisdom says that keeping distributions from portfolios to 4 percent or less is the best way to give your portfolio the best chance to not run out of money. While it is a good idea, there are a number of problems with this statement and the conventional wisdom. The first problem is that there is no such thing as a sure thing. Even if a person is taking nothing out of the portfolio, it's possible to substantially lose money being in the market, particularly over short periods of time. There are other factors that can similarly eviscerate the value of a portfolio.

Imagine a time of hyperinflation. This is where the value of a dollar may be decreasing by triple digits year over year. It sounds crazy, right? Well, this is what happened in Brazil. At points in the late 1980s/early 1990s, inflation was at quadruple digits. Imagine being a Brazilian bank accountholder or bondholder at that time. The value of your accounts were decimated.

It happened there; it could happen here. We may feel immune to it because we've had historically low inflation over the last decade, but everything is cyclical, and our parents who secured mortgages in the early 1980s at 15 percent could tell us a bit about the yin of this current inflation yang. So when I warn of losing your money without spending a dime, I'm talking about inflation and interest rate risk, which is real. Taking 4 percent of a portfolio of bond ladders is a good way to lose all your money over a long period of time. The combination of withdrawals plus inflation has the potential of destroying a retirement plan.

Thus, the conventional wisdom really needs to be relabeled: Take 4 percent of a diversified portfolio that includes a healthy amount in stocks, and you likely won't run out of money. Even that phrasing, however, has its own problems. Why 4 percent? What happens if we take 5 percent or 6 percent? What about 10 percent?

The problem is that when we use general rules, they by definition don't work for everybody. It's also fairly inflexible. There is constant research about how to best tailor distribution models for those drawing an income. Larry Frank has authored and co-authored a number of articles that explore going beyond the conventional wisdom.

In an article that was published in the November 2016 edition of the FPA Journal, he and Shawn Brayman go through painstaking modeling to try to come up with a better way to determine rates of withdrawal. What they eventually find is that withdrawal rates have to be adjusted for life expectancy and actual rates of return. While being older generally means you are permitted a higher rate of withdrawal, if the markets don't cooperate, you'll have to adjust expectations.

Taking Some Off the Table and Then Putting It Back On: The Importance of Rebalancing

At some point, every one of my clients looks at me with bewilderment, and it's almost always over the same thing: rebalancing. Over the course of our lifetimes, there are dips in the market. Some are relatively small (less than 10 percent), some are slightly bigger and are called corrections (over 10 percent), and some are downright catastrophic (a fall of greater than 40 percent). I don't like it when the market goes down; it makes my job exceptionally difficult.

For one thing, there is nothing I can do about the market going down. As explained in previous chapters, market timing does not work either on the buying or the selling end. The other part that makes my job difficult is that I am forced into becoming a psychologist. In the behavioral finance part of this book, we went through how our brains make us bad investors. When the market seemingly falls off a cliff, clients start talking crazy. It's my job to make sure that they don't do real damage to themselves. (Note: This is probably the main reason why you need to pay an advisor and one of the many areas where robo-advisors fall short.)

It's also my job to take advantage of an opportunity. When the stock market tanks, that means that almost all stocks are lower than they were before they tanked. It's a truism, if there ever has been one. Logically, if stocks are a relative bargain, an investor should buy. The opposite side of the coin is true. If the market has been climbing to an all-time high, investors should be looking to take some of their gains off the table and bank them.

This goes against our intuitions as human beings. Our brains are wired to seek pleasurable situations and avoid painful ones. A stock market that is crashing is a painful experience: it hurts us right in the pocketbook. An upward trending market is sometimes described as euphoric. We see our net worth go up, and it feels good. Thus, we want to stop the pain of a fall and prolong the feelings of going up.

I like to rain on everybody's parade. As mentioned previously, a well-balanced portfolio has some bonds to help dampen volatility. Because the better risk-adjusted returns historically occur in the stock market, short-term high-quality bonds have the desired stability to offset market volatility. Historically, these bonds don't move a lot in either direction. This lack of movement makes having bonds an important arrow in the portfolio quiver.

When the market plummets and the bonds stay relatively steady, a very predictable thing happens to a portfolio: The stocks become under-weighted (because they are falling in price), and the bonds become over-weighted (because their price stays steady). If an investor is trying to keep a certain risk level in the portfolio, this would mean they are not taking enough risk.

For example, a person who is 60 percent in the stock market and 40 percent in bonds sees a sizeable shift in their portfolio if the market falls by 15 percent. Their 60 percent in the market becomes 56 percent in the market, and their bond holdings go to 44 percent. A fall by 30 percent shifts the portfolio to 51 percent in the market, 49 percent in bonds. By not rebalancing, the client could be missing out on a real opportunity.

This is at the core of the crazy looks clients give me when I tell them in the middle of a bloodbath that I want to sell their safety net and buy more of the blood bath; or when the market is really cooking that I want to turn down the heat by selling the part of the portfolio that is doing really well and buying the part that is barely moving. Nevertheless, for someone wanting to maintain their risk level, these are the right moves to make.

People who are pulling money out of their portfolios for living expenses still need to take advantage of this fact. It is key to producing better returns over time. Take the 20-year period between January 1, 2006, and December 31, 2015. If an investor had a basic portfolio of 50 percent in the S&P 500, 40 percent EAFE, and 10 percent MSCI Emerging Markets, they would have seen a benefit in rebalancing. A portfolio rebalanced at the end of every year for ten years yielded an annual rate of return of 5.49 percent. A portfolio

Rebalancing Matters

Rebalancing a 50% Stocks / 50% Bonds Portfolio — 1998 to 2017

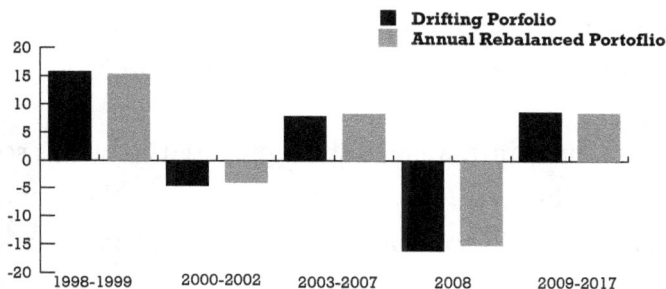

Legend:
- ■ Drifting Porfolio
- ■ Annual Rebalanced Portoflio

	1 year	3 years	5 years	10 years	20 years	20 year standard deviation
Drifting Portfolio Annual Return (%)	14.0	7.56	9.55	5.88	5.66	7.08
Rebalanced Portfolio Annual Return (%)	11.48	6.38	8.62	5.90	5.85	7.04

All investments involve risk, including loss of principal.[1]

that was not rebalanced over that same period of time would have returned 5.07 percent.

These kinds of exercises are nice, but at the end of the day, you can't invest in an index directly, and past performance doesn't guarantee future results. It illustrates the importance of rebalancing over long periods of time.

Taking 10 Percent From Your Portfolio Annually—Wanna Party?

I spend a lot of time planning with clients. Sometimes, even with Social Security, I am forced to push a portfolio to its boundaries.

This usually means somewhere around a 6 percent withdrawal rate. My clients are always warned that this will put high stress on a portfolio and that there may come a time when the market falters significantly and that 6 percent will become 7 percent or 8 percent. When those points are reached, it will be time to cut back.

Every client assures me that he or she is prepared for such a scenario. Around six months later, I receive a phone call from the client. They tell me that they need to pull out another $5,000 to pay for a "special vacation." Six months after that I get another call for another $5,000 to pay for a grandchild's tuition. The 6 percent withdrawal rate does not last for long.

There are some clients who seemingly have a constant level of tzuris (Yiddish for problems) and end up at a 10 percent withdrawal rate. And occasionally, that 10 percent becomes systematized through monthly withdrawals. Admittedly, some clients do this because they end up in a long-term care scenario (which we'll talk about later on in this chapter). But spending assets down at a 10 percent rate usually yields horrific results.

The main problem is due to the math. Let's say a client has a $1 million portfolio. For whatever reason, they need $100,000 per year to live, and the portfolio earns 6 percent per year. The effective withdrawal rate increases every year, and the stress on the portfolio builds until there is no more money left. Here is a chart explaining the concept:

Year	Beginning Principal	Return	Withdrawal	Ending Principal	Rate of Withdrawal
1	1,000,000.00	60,000.00	100,000.00	960,000.00	10.00%
2	960,000.00	57,600.00	100,000.00	917,600.00	10.42%
3	917,600.00	55,056.00	100,000.00	872,656.00	10.90%
4	872,656.00	52,359.36	100,000.00	825,015.36	11.46%
5	825,015.36	49,500.92	100,000.00	774,516.28	12.12%
6	774,516.28	46,470.98	100,000.00	720,987.26	12.91%
7	720,987.26	43,259.24	100,000.00	664,246.49	13.87%
8	664,246.49	39,854.79	100,000.00	604,101.28	15.05%
9	604,101.28	36,246.08	100,000.00	540,347.36	16.55%
10	540,347.36	32,420.84	100,000.00	472,768.20	18.51%
11	472,768.20	28,366.09	100,000.00	401,134.29	21.15%
12	401,134.29	24,068.06	100,000.00	325,202.35	24.93%
13	325,202.35	19,512.14	100,000.00	244,714.49	30.75%
14	244,714.49	14,682.87	100,000.00	159,397.36	40.86%
15	159,397.36	9,563.84	100,000.00	68,961.20	62.74%
16	68,961.20	4,137.67	100,000.00	(26,901.12)	145.01%

In case you were wondering, having a negative net worth at the end of Year 16 is bad. Truth be told, this is the best-case scenario! This is assuming that all of the return happens in the beginning of the year, and the withdrawal happens at the end of the year. It also assumes a constant 6 percent rate of return for 16 years, which has never happened in the history of the S&P 500. If you factor in a correction every three to four years, 16 years is a complete pipe dream.

The Financial Drain of Long-Term Care (CODA)

Want to burn through all your assets as quickly as possible? End up in a long-term care situation. I already discussed the mechanics behind long-term care in Chapter 5, but I didn't really go through the impacts that long-term care has on life.

The issue with ending up in a long-term care scenario, whether it be assisted living or nursing care, is that it affects the whole family. The first, and possibly worst, family impact is recognizing that your loved one is unable to take care of himself or herself. Even worse, in many situations the parent—the one who raised you, loved you, and was overjoyed with grandkids—is slipping away into the abyss of dementia or other psychological/physical impairment.

To compound this problem, many people specify to loved ones that they do not want to be removed from their home. When they are well, they cannot fathom being in a nursing facility, and the thought of that situation is downright scary. All this does is put pressure on the family not to move the person out of his or her home, even when staying in the home is impractical or impossible.

I have seen some bad situations where the parent was living in conditions that were unacceptable and would be unacceptable to anyone who had all of their faculties in place. Maintaining a home eventually becomes an impossibility. Repairs that must be made are ignored, and cleanliness deteriorates. However, the family is reticent to change the living conditions because the parent was so insistent on staying at home.

I have seen this situation get to the extreme where a family member will move in with the loved one for a period of months or even years. This puts a strain on sibling relationships, and nearly inevitably, there ends up being mistrust—sometimes justified. That tension becomes intergenerational when grandchildren move in with grandparents. Many times, the caretaker is the one who is serially unemployed and may not be the most financially savvy.

But what really pulls everything apart is the money. In my experience in the Bay Area, many families are in sticker shock when they see that assisted living could be between $6,000 and $8,000 per month. Consider that the senior's bills prior to this were around $1,000 per month. It quickly becomes obvious that Social Security will not cover this expense. Medicare doesn't cover very much either.

For those with less, they must do without. This means that there is a high likelihood that they will not receive the care they need because they are stuck. Many will end up at the homes of children or other relatives. Again, this adds to the strain that families go through and may not increase the level of care that the senior receives.

Nursing care is the next level up. If you're like me and you love baseball, assisted living is the minor leagues and nursing care is the majors. There is no comparison to the level of care. Typically, people in this scenario may be unable to feed themselves, bathe themselves, or toilet themselves.

Nursing care can easily run as much as $15,000 per month, at least for my clients. If the person does not have a long-term care policy (see Chapter 5), the rest of the money has to come from somewhere. Medicaid is the plan of last resort. To get on Medicaid, a person basically has to spend through their money. They have to be truly destitute. They have to have almost no cash, little house value, and have exhausted almost every other resource to apply. If you want to gift money to kids, think again. There is a five-year look-back period, which limits these types of workarounds. Even worse, because Medicaid pays so little on the dollar, many nursing homes will severely limit the number of Medicaid beds. If you find your loved one in a Medicaid situation, it may be worth your while to find a good elder law attorney, especially if the facility ends up playing games. (Note: In California, the rules for Medi-Cal are different.)

The Ray of Hope

What is the best way not to run out of money? Have enough of it when you retire. (Aren't you glad you bought this book?) The bottom 50 percent of incomes in the United States average $35,000 per year and have almost no retirement savings. This means that many people end up having to retire with very little and most definitely not enough to sustain a prolonged withdrawal period.

This doesn't mean that they need to start eating cat food, but it does mean that there will be sacrifices to make. While there is no silver bullet that can fix the problem of not having enough, there are a few conventional ways to make retirement happen, and a few more unconventional ones.

Getting Your Own Money Back

Remember when you had your first crappy job back in high school? Perhaps you were working a fast food job or restocking for a retail store (which I did). It sucked, and you got paid maybe $8 an hour. We all knew it going in, but we all longed for the paycheck, which, if we worked full-time, would be $640 every other week. It was enough to cover gas, insurance, and a car payment, which is what most of us needed it for.

Do you also remember the draining disappointment of receiving your first paycheck? There were all kinds of acronyms on there: FIT, SIT, FICA, SDI, and perhaps more, depending on where you're from. The reality that your $640 paycheck ended up being $450 was positively deflating. Thankfully, one of those acronyms—FICA (Federal Insurance Contributions Act)—may pay off. FICA includes Social Security.

The most powerful tool in the conventional track is Social Security. Social Security cannot solve all financial problems, but it acts as a backstop and can be used to layer on additional cash flows. To be eligible for Social Security, you need to have worked 40 quarters, or around 10 years, in which you made more than around $5,000 annually.

The Social Security calculation begins with your earnings history. From the time you start working until the time you retire, your benefit is derived from how much you contributed to the system. How much you put in is determined by how much you make. There is a maximum wage for Social Security purposes, and it increases with inflation.

You have a number of options on how to collect Social Security. Based upon the year you were born, everybody has a full retirement age (FRA). The FRA is the age at which recipients receive the full benefits as calculated by their work history.

Retiring at the FRA is not required. For most people, the earliest age you can retire is age 62. However, if retiring prior to reaching the FRA, the retiree will not receive the full benefits but rather a percentage thereof. For every month prior to the FRA, benefits are reduced by 0.55 percent per month to 0.42 percent depending on when a person chooses to retire.

The other side of that coin is that it is possible to wait past the FRA to take benefits. Those who delay can earn an additional 8 percent per year on their monthly benefit, up until age 70. Once a retiree turns 70, they cannot accrue any additional benefit. So the longer someone can wait to claim benefits, the better off they are on a monthly cash flow basis. Of course, if the money is needed now to pay rent, waiting isn't a good option.

This is all great in theory. However, my belief is that anyone under the age of 50 needs to plan gingerly with Social Security. The problem is that Social Security is fundamentally a Ponzi scheme at this point. Remember how people used to only have five to 10 years in retirement? Having the younger generation pay for them wasn't a big deal. However, as people live longer and longer and our population demographic gets older and older, the numbers simply don't pencil out.

My guess is that there is going to be a means test one day. Those who make more than a certain amount (your guess is as good as mine as to that number) will have reduced benefits. Social Security will be in place, but only for a certain percentage of the population. Will that include you? Only time will tell, but the conservative thing to do is to open your Social Security statement, laugh, and forget about it.

Mortgaging (or Possibly Selling) Your Future

We often think of being house-poor as a problem that a young person has. Conventional wisdom says to buy the biggest (best) house you can afford. Maxing out your house budget means sacrificing on other things. Because a house is likely to increase in value, it's not a bad bet and can be something worth sacrificing for.

However, it's not just a young person's problem anymore. Increasingly, seniors end up in financial positions where their home is their asset of last resort. The question becomes what to do if you find yourself or your loved one in such a place. The answer is that it depends on the circumstance of the person.

If the retiree is relatively young and in good health, moving is not a bad option. It's important to look at the tax consequences. If the person is single and the gain is less than $250,000 (if married: $500,000), they'll be able to take the net proceeds tax-free (Federal income tax). They can do anything they want with the cash: use it for assisted living, rent, or to buy a less expensive house.

The goal is to maximize the remaining cash such that the retiree can create a sustainable cash flow. This may entail getting a small loan on a new property. If the retiree can get a loan for $100,000 or $200,000, the loan payment may just be a few hundred dollars a month. If they can generate more in cash flow from investing those funds, it's better to arbitrage, or take advantage of the difference in interest rates.

There are lots of reasons to use loans (also called leverage). For me, loans should be limited to acquisitions of assets likely to appreciate in value (real estate) or expenses likely to generate more revenue than the original outlay (business loans). However, there comes a time where loans can become a critical piece of cash flow.

If the retiree is getting older and is concerned about large unforeseen expenses, the right decision may be to get a home equity line of credit (HELOC). An HELOC is a bit like opening a checking account using your house. The checks that you write are rolled into a running balance mortgage. The loans are usually interest-only. There is typically a limit on an HELOC of around $250,000, but the value of the home and monthly income play a big part in determining the cap.

The benefit of an HELOC is that you only use it when you need it. A mortgagee can keep a zero balance and never owe a cent of interest. This is perfect for the retiree who only needs the money in case of a big emergency. However, there are drawbacks. An HELOC typically has a draw period of ten years. This means that after ten years, the HELOC goes into a payoff period (meaning you can no longer draw), or is closed or refinanced. It's possible that a retiree won't be able to refinance if the value of the house or cash flows fall.

For me, the loan of last resort is the reverse mortgage, also euphemistically called a home equity conversion mortgage (HECM). In full disclosure, I am not a reverse mortgage expert. I know a few mortgage brokers who make their whole careers by touting and writing reverse mortgages. To be fair, reverse mortgages have come a long way. They used to be prohibitively expensive and quite confusing. They're much more reasonable in cost nowadays and a bit less confusing.

The big picture is that a lender is going to lend you money using your home as collateral. In a traditional mortgage, you pay the bank for the house, but in a reverse, the bank pays you for the house. In this way, a reverse mortgage works somewhat like an HELOC. Your home is collateral, you pull money out, and the bank charges you interest on what you take out. However, unlike an HELOC, the limitations aren't as low.

In order to qualify for a reverse mortgage, the mortgagee has to be at least 62 years old. As to how much someone can take out of their home, well, that's a bit more complicated. It's really a function of the borrower's age, the interest rate, appraised value, and the maximum lending limit. There are also different types of reverse mortgages, which are lump sum, monthly payments, or line of credit.

The problem is that all of these factors interplay with one another. The older the applicant, the greater percentage he or she can take out of the home. The lower the interest rate, the more can be taken out; the higher the appraised value, the more can be taken out. Put a cap on the program imposed by Federal Housing Authority (FHA), and you have a continuum. There are some lenders that offer non-FHA loans. In these programs, the caps may be much higher. However, they can be more expensive and more complicated, so be extra careful.

When a reverse mortgage is done via lump sum, the limit that a 62-year-old can get is 45 percent of the value of the home. No matter what the property value, the maximum mortgage limit is

$625,000 for an FHA loan. Your home can be worth $5 million; it doesn't matter. The line of credit option is interesting. Basically, you get a reverse mortgage on the house, but you don't take any money. As the loan lies fallow, the amount you can take grows. You still have to pay closing costs and fees.

The potential benefit to a reverse mortgage is that the person gets a lifeline of cash, either monthly, paid out in a lump sum, or accessed whenever needed. The other benefit is that person doesn't have to pay back the mortgage during his or her lifetime. Instead, the interest accrues and gets capitalized into the loan. When the person ultimately passes away, if the loan is worth more than the home, the house is sold and the lender does not collect any additional proceeds.

The downsides are numerous. First, there is opening the reverse mortgage. There are a number of fees to take into consideration. There is an origination fee, which can be as much as $6,000 depending on the size of the mortgage. To be fair, there are also similar fees to getting a traditional mortgage: appraisal, survey, title, and credit checks.

There is also a mortgage insurance premium (MIP). As I mentioned, if the house ends up going underwater, the mortgagee and family will not be out of pocket anything additional. That's because FHA comes in and takes the bath. They don't take that bath out of the kindness of their hearts but rather act as insurance. The mortgagee is responsible for paying an insurance premium to FHA. There is an up-front premium, which ranges from 0.50 percent to 2.5 percent, and an ongoing premium that is credited against the mortgage at least annually.

Then there is the issue of interest rates. The only way to get a fixed rate is to take the lump sum option. Once you take your lump sum, there is no going back unless you end up being able to get a new reverse mortgage to pay off the old one. This may be a difficult prospect. The original reverse mortgage may have gone up substantially due to interest being capitalized and compounded. The rates are higher than what you would normally pay a bank for a loan, but not credit card high. Typically, the rates are set to a benchmark (prime, Libor, etc.), and then a premium is tacked on top.

Additionally, there are a few requirements: Real estate tax must be paid by the mortgagee, and the mortgagee must be living in the house. If either of these two conditions are not met, the mortgagee is in default and must immediately pay back the loan or sell the house. If the senior ends up in assisted living or nursing care, the game is over. The options are the same as when the person passes away. The beneficiaries can pay back the reverse mortgage company, or they can sell the home and receive whatever remains of the proceeds.

Check, Please!

You are likely many years away from downsizing and retirement at this point in your life, but time flies as you're no doubt discovering. To avoid approaching retirement completely unprepared, keep the following tips in mind:

1. **Plan on living a long time.** This means that you need to have a lot of money saved up to sustain yourself for what will likely be a 30-year retirement.

2. **Use 4 percent as a guideline.** As you plan for retirement, the conservative estimate on how much you can safely withdraw from a given portfolio is around 4%. Of course, you'll need to take market risk to sustain that level of drawdown.

3. **Pushing a portfolio to the edge means that in downturns, you'll have to cut back.** Continuing heavy distributions during falling markets is a surefire way to run out of money.

4. **If you find yourself nearing retirement without much to show for it and you can no longer work, there are other options.** Start with the least painful one, like Social Security and then see if you can build upon that.

5. **If you need to use your home to fund your retirement, consider moving or downsizing if taxation permits.** Your last option should be a reverse mortgage, but as long as you go in understanding the limitations and pitfalls, it can be an effective tool.

Endnote

! All investments involve risk, including loss of principal. Data Source: Morningstar Direct. Past performance is no indication of future results. Stocks are represented by the S&P 500 Index. Bonds are represented by Citi WGBI 1-5 Yr Hedged USD index. Indexes are unmanaged baskets of securities in which investors cannot invest and they do not reflect the payment of advisory fees associated with a mutual fund or separate account. Returns assume dividend and capital gain reinvestment. Stock investing involves risks, including increased volatility (up and down movement in the value of your assets) and loss of principal. Bonds are subject to market and interest rate risk. Bond values will decline as interest rates rise, issuer's creditworthiness declines, and are subject to availability and changes in price.

Performance shown is not representative of the performance of any Loring Ward portfolio and does not represent the experience of any Loring Ward client. Past performance is no guarantee of future results.

CHAPTER 10

Philanthropist: Another Name for Old Rich Dude (or Dudette)

My first memories of charitable giving revolve around my synagogue. One of the very first things that Jewish children are taught in Hebrew School (often referred to as "Religious School") is the concept of tzedukah, a Hebrew word most often misidentified to mean charity.

The misidentification stems from the fact that charity is a terrible translation. The Bible does not merely suggest that people give 10 percent of their income; it is compulsory.

Charity suggests something much more optional. A person can feel charitable in any instant and give, or perhaps the instant passes and the person doesn't give. Charity is fickle. When the economy tanks, charity dries up. Thus, tzedukah bears a resemblance to charity in the same way I bear resemblance to Tom Brady. One is a higher order creature than the other. Sorry, Tom, but one day maybe you can be me.

While tzedukah changed my outlook on obligations to others and the community, it isn't really philanthropy. A philanthropist is more than just a giver of funds. He or she is a patron, a benefactor, someone who doesn't merely fund projects but entire movements. The philantropist's giving isn't haughty or showy, yet their presence is always well known.

I recall walking into synagogue with my mother on Rosh Hashanah (one of the most important holidays of the Jewish year) when I was seven or eight years old. Our synagogue's membership was much bigger than the capacity of the sanctuary. Actually, that's not entirely true. Like our Christian brethren, Jewish people have two days a year where nearly 100 percent of people will show up. For Christians, those two days are Christmas and Easter. For Jews, those two days are Rosh Hashanah and Yom Kippur. All other days of the year, almost nobody shows.

Growing up, my synagogue was the up and comer, and on those two days of the year, the enormous social hall made an extension of the sanctuary, and later on, the doors outside of the sanctuary were opened, and the patio tented, to make room for even more seating.

The first choice was always the main sanctuary. The chairs were padded, roomy, and had places to store your books. The second choice was the social hall. Those chairs had worse padding, no book storage, but it was air-conditioned. The worst choice by far was the tent. The chairs were bad, you were on top of cement, book storage was a pipe dream, and if a heat wave hit in early September, you'd bake at the same time.

As a child, I was perplexed by the fact that we always sat in the social hall. From my perspective we had always been members of the congregation, so why did we never sit in the main sanctuary? When I asked my mother the question, she told me, "That's where the machers sit." For those unfamiliar with that particular Yiddish term, a macher is a person of significance, a mover and shaker. They also typically give a lot of money.

And while all machers are not philanthropists, all philanthropists are machers. From my youth, I identified those who gave heavily as those with status. As I became more involved with the inner workings of synagogues, I realized there was more than one way to become a macher, but giving impactful monetary gifts makes people bend over backwards for you.

The Quick and Dirty on Estate Planning Documents

I once had a young power couple in my office. He was a successful sales director, and she was an entrepreneur. They came into my office with a stock option problem. As we met for the first time, we went through all of their investment accounts, all of the option vesting periods, talked about the tax implication of exercising different types of options, and came up with a net worth of around $10 million. They also had two gifted young children, ages eight and ten.

They also had no will, no trust, and no power of attorney. No estate plan at all.

While they may have had a stock option problem, they had an even bigger estate planning problem. What would happen to their assets if they died unexpectedly? What would happen to their children? The answer went something like this:

If you die without a written plan, the state has a plan for you, and you're not going to like it. It's called probate. Probate is a process where a judge clears title to the property owned by a decedent (a.k.a. the dead person).

Absent a will, your stuff has to go somewhere. By "your stuff" I mean your house, dog, pots, pans, artwork, car, tax refund, bank accounts, and anything else that has value. Who gets your stuff is determined by the laws of intestacy. Generally, the law (which is different in every state) says that if you are married with no kids, your spouse gets your stuff. If you are married and have kids, your stuff gets split between your spouse and kids. If you have no spouse but do have kids, then it all goes to your kids. If you have neither a spouse nor kids, it goes to your parents. If no parents, then siblings.

It keeps going to more and more distant relatives until you run out of relatives. Once out of relatives, your property escheats to the state in which you live. The state then sells your stuff and keeps the proceeds to fund whatever nefarious, wasteful government program some bureaucrat who has never had a real job finds most politically convenient.

You may be thinking to yourself that my clients would have died and their stuff would have gone to their kids. Perhaps, but who would have custody of the children? If they have no documents, the Court doesn't know who to award custody to. Some judge who has a full caseload and needs to clear his docket before going to Hawaii is going to decide which person is best suited to take care of your kids. If you have a judge, that means you have lawyers involved. If you have lawyers involved, that means your estate is being spent down paying lawyers and court costs.

I had a friend whose family member had lived with someone for over thirty years. Everyone thought that they were married. As it turned out, they were not. When the not-spouse spouse died, everyone was surprised to learn that he didn't have a will. The problem was that he was the sole owner of the house, and she didn't have any significant assets of her own. The result was that house went to the deceased person's sister who then generously agreed to give the house to my friend's family member. They spent plenty of money on attorneys when a will would have made everything a lot easier.

However, wills are subject to probate as well. Wills tell the Court where you want your stuff to go, but they are still subject to the probate process. Every state has different rules when it comes to wills, so use your state bar website if you have questions, or go to an estate planning attorney. The benefit of a will is that it gives the court direction. It tells the Court who you want to manage your estate's affairs, and it even lets the Court know who should be the guardians of your children.

If you die with a will, your executor (the person who you nominated to be in charge) takes your will to the courthouse, files paperwork, and then gets a letter of administration that lets them access all of your accounts and transact on the assets. The assets are sold or distributed by the executor. The Court has oversight over your executor, and so your executor may have to provide court accountings and may need an attorney to help. In the end, a will can still be expensive depending on the size and complexity of the estate.

The most efficient way to have your estate managed is via trust. A trust is a document that, like a will, tells what you want to have happen to your stuff. That's where the similarities of trusts and wills end. A trust not only deals with your assets when you die but also talks about your assets while you are alive. Should you be unable to manage your affairs due to illness or incapacity, the trust appoints someone to take over on your behalf.

A trust has three basic parts:

1. Trustee: the person who runs the trust

2. Beneficiary: the person whom the trust benefits

3. Corpus: the stuff inside of the trust

If a trust doesn't have all of these three things, it is not a trust. Normally, people create living trusts. A living trust is revocable, which means that it can be changed or done away with entirely at any time. In a living trust, the person who created the trust (also called the grantor), is the trustee and beneficiary, so they remain in complete control.

The grantor names a successor trustee, so there is someone to take over when the grantor dies or becomes incapacitated. When the grantor ultimately dies, the successor trustee is going to distribute the money according to the terms of the trust. Perhaps there is a child with special needs. In that case, the trust can hold those assets in a special-needs trust that is controlled by a trustee for the child's benefit during the child's lifetime.

The real benefit of a trust is that it is not subject to court oversight. When a trustee wants access to an account, they simply present the trust document and proof they are in power as the trustee. What if you forget to put an asset inside of a trust? That's why you still need a will, often referred to as a pour-over will. The will acts as a catchall and collects assets that fell through the cracks; it basically turns the assets over to the trust. Your will is also the main vehicle for telling the Court about your children's guardian.

Generally, there is no need for probate attorneys with trusts, so costs are much lower for estate administration. The downside is that you need to pay an attorney to set up the trust, which is going to cost some up-front money—figure somewhere between $1,500 and $2,000. Whether you are reading the book via paper or e-reader, I need you to raise your right hand and say these words out loud. I don't care if everyone on the train thinks you're crazy:

I, <your name>, swear I will not use some estate planning mill where I got a free dinner and a crappy presentation to do my will and/or trust. Furthermore, I will not try to do my own estate plan by myself. LegalZoom is great, but my children and family are too important to me to be a cheapskate.

That is all.

The final estate planning documents to talk about are powers of attorney and living wills. While many of us were still young at the time, we may recall the story of Terry Schiavo. Terry was a young woman in Florida (thanks again, Florida) who was walking down the hall of her apartment and fell over unconscious for unknown reasons. After she was rushed to the hospital, it was quickly determined that she was basically brain-dead but able to breathe.

Terry's husband tried his best to see if there was any way to bring her back, but there wasn't. He was appointed her guardian, and he ordered her feeding tube removed, which would eventually end her life.

There was one problem. There were no documents that said she wanted to be removed from lifesaving technology, and her parents were not ready to give up. So they ran to the courthouse with an injunction to put the tube back in. The judge granted the injunction. Though Terry's death had been stopped, a multi-year legal battle that sucked in the country began. Eventually, Congress would pass a bill that interloped in the Schiavo case.

Here's my legal analysis: When your estate plan involves an act of Congress, it's a bad plan. Eventually, Terry Schiavo's feeding tube did get removed, and she did pass away peacefully. But she could have saved her family hundreds of thousands of dollars in legal bills had she merely written down her wishes. With this in mind, there are a few documents that every person in the United States should have regardless of age or economic status:

1. Medical power of attorney

2. Durable financial power of attorney

3. Living will

Your medical power of attorney (POA) is going to give a third party the authorization to make medical decisions on your behalf should you be unable to do so. If you get into a car accident and are unconscious, your medical POA will give the go-ahead for surgeries. It's generally good to have a medical POA who has some background in medicine and knows you well enough to make decisions that you would make.

A financial POA gives a person the ability to make non-medical decisions for you in the case of your incapacity. Taking the car accident example again, while you are in the hospital unable to make decisions for yourself, you still need to pay your rent, credit card, car payment, and lots of other items. Your financial POA is going to take care of that for you. That person can walk into a bank with the document and prove you're incapacitated and do transactions on your behalf. Note: Once you are dead, POAs have no effect. They only work during your lifetime. Once you have died, that's when your wills and trusts start to kick in.

There are some important things to note about the financial power of attorney. They come in a couple of different flavors, so pick your flavor wisely. First, they can be durable or non-durable. A durable power of attorney survives incapacity, meaning that if you can't make decisions for yourself, it's still active. A non-durable is the opposite; once you become incapacitated, the person with the power loses it. If your goal is to make sure you can pay your bills during incapacity, you want a durable POA.

A POA can also be either springing or non-springing. A springing power of attorney only goes into effect when you are incapacitated. A non-springing power of attorney goes into effect immediately. While there are good reasons to have a non-springing power of attorney, for estate planning purposes you mainly want a springing POA. In sum, make sure (especially if you do it on your own) you have a durable springing power of attorney.

Finally, living wills could have saved Terry Schiavo's family a lot of heartache. Your living will says what you want to have happen at the end stages of your life. It takes the decision-making out of your POA's hands and lets you call the shots. You get to say whether you want life support, a feeding tube, or any other life-extending measure. If you are the type of person who wants to lay in bed unresponsive, hey, that's cool. I'm not judging (okay, I'm judging a little), but it's your decision. Did Terry Schiavo want to be a vegetable? Nobody will ever know, but I'm nearly certain she didn't want her family burning through hundreds of thousands of dollars on court battles.

Enjoying Giving While You Are Alive (a.k.a. Making People Kiss Your Keister)

I knew of a client who felt very strongly about his alma mater, and for him, he could not imagine a world in which he did not leave a bulk of his estate to that institution. So he gave the school a million dollars . . . kind of. He didn't write a check to the development department; rather, he made a specific bequest to the university inside of a charitable remainder unit trust (CRUT—more on the mechanics later in this section). In essence, the school wouldn't get the money until he died. That way, the school couldn't just forget about him.

In many charitable-type trusts, the trustee has the power to change the beneficiary. Perhaps the trustee cannot dissolve the trust, but the power to change is almost as good. The charity knows that it cannot piss off the grantor, and they need to continually court the grantor in case another organization comes along gunning to be the ultimate beneficiary.

The client who had the trust was constantly being pinged by his alma mater. Every season he was offered complimentary football tickets, special dinners with the president of the college, and lots of recognition. Not that it was the client's prime reason, but he did enjoy all of the attention. Had he kept his CRUT silent or just had a provision in his will or living trust, he would have had his name in the back of a development magazine when he died. It's more fun to have development officers fawn all over you when you're still here.

How do you accomplish this? First, have the assets do it (see Chapters 1–9 of this book). Second, use the correct transfer vehicle.

Estate Tax in a Paragraph

At this point, there are probably very few people who are worrying about estate tax. Talking about the effects of estate tax is like talking about the effects of the Chupacabra—it doesn't do many people good. If you are one of those people, I'd love to work with you, so call me. For the rest of us, the individual exemption for estate tax in 2019 is $11.4 million (indexed for inflation), or $22.8 million for a married couple, so 99.9 percent of the country doesn't have to think twice. There is one quirk to know about: If your spouse dies before you, and it is possible that when you die you'll have more than $11.4 million, you need to file an estate tax return and elect portability. Portability allows you to carry over your spouse's exemption to your own estate tax return for future use. Failing to elect portability could result in the government getting a big chunk of money when the second spouse passes away. Don't let the Chupacabra get you!

Show Me the Money!

The starting point to be considered a macher is a person's goals. If the goal is to give $10,000, you don't need a lot of fancy legal structures. Truth be told, with $10,000, there aren't a whole lot of organizations that will send you swag. It isn't such an insignificant sum that organizations will ignore you, but don't expect football tickets to the big game from your alma mater.

Since we are not talking about big bucks, what you might be better off doing is working with a donor advised fund (DAF). When you donate money to a DAF, you are taking a full tax deduction of what you put in now, and you can spread the money over multiple organizations over a period of years. So the $10,000 might take a couple of years to spend down depending on your level of giving.

The mechanics of a DAF are straightforward. First, a person finds an umbrella organization. Bigger organizations that typically support other organizations in the community will have DAFs available at little to no charge. Typically, large faith-based institutions will run them so that they can spread around the money to all of the other smaller causes that they support. National Christian Foundation operates one, as does Jewish Federation. Custodians such as Charles Schwab or Fidelity have non-faith-based DAFs as well.

It's important to know that the umbrella legally has the funds and can technically spend it any way they like. This is the main issue that donors have with a DAF. The word "advised" connotes that the group running the fund does not have to listen to the person who put the money into the account. While this is legally accurate, in practice, the organization would never do such a thing. Once word gets out that a donor's money was effectively commandeered by the umbrella organization, no one would ever use their DAF again.

One of the potential benefits (in terms of keister kissing) is that the larger umbrella charity knows what money you have left in the account. This means you can have meetings with the organization in deciding what money should go where, and you may get some invitations to events. For many organizations, $10,000 does not represent a large amount, so keep your expectations low.

Giving and Showing the Love

Many people prefer the old-fashioned way of giving money: writing a check to a single organization. That's cool. However, the modern millennial needs to rethink this strategy. While giving a check is effective, it only really kills one bird with its stone. To kill two birds, a taxpayer should use their highly appreciated stock.

When an individual sells his appreciated stock, he has to pay capital gains tax. This tax can range from 0 percent to 23.8 percent Federal, and then you may have to tack on state income tax. This is not an ideal situation. Qualified charitable organizations pay 0 percent tax, and so the stock you give stretches further because the taxman is effectively cut out.

Here's the rub: Your deduction of the appreciated stock is limited to 30 percent of your adjusted gross income (AGI). So if you make $200,000 in income for the year, you can deduct up to $60,000 of the stock donation in the current year. Any amount in excess must be carried forward (up to five years) and is subject to the 30 percent cap every year. Cash donations are not subject to the same rule. With cash donations, you can deduct up to 60 percent of AGI.

The opposite side of that coin is having stock in a loss position. NEVER GIVE STOCK IN A LOSS POSITION. Sell the stock, reap the capital loss for your own tax return, and give the cash to the organization. Because the organization can't use the loss, it is far more tax-efficient for an individual to recognize the loss for themselves.

CRUTs: As Easy As A-B-C (Not Really)

If you don't mind giving away assets but would like to maintain an income stream, a charitable remainder unit trust (CRUT) is a good candidate. You start by putting an appreciated asset inside of the trust. This could be real property, securities, or some other financial interest. You (and most of the time your spouse) will get a stated income stream, based upon a percentage of assets annually, over your lifetime. Once both income beneficiaries pass away, whatever is left generally goes to the named charity. As a trustee, you are allowed to change the charity, hence the ability to score football tickets.

CRUTs are more expensive animals. First, you need to create it, and depending on the complexity this can range from $2,000 to $5,000. But costs don't end there. Once a trust is established for charitable purposes, there are compliance costs.

Every year, the trust is going to have to file its own income tax return. Most people aren't comfortable—and rightly so—with preparing a trust return by themselves, and that means paying a preparer. Depending on the asset, there may be bookkeeping or other accounting costs. That being said, a basket of marketable securities is a bit simpler than a multi-unit apartment building, making a tax return less expensive to prepare.

Despite the costs, people use CRUTs mainly to avoid massive capital gains. Most people choose to fund CRUTs with highly appreciated assets because the taxable gain, though realized, is not immediately recognized when sold inside of a CRUT. The gain remains inside of the CRUT and gets distributed over time.

How quickly this gain gets distributed boils down to the tax mechanics. If a CRUT is required to pay 7 percent of assets as income every year, the first part of the distribution is funded by current income (dividends and interest in the case of a CRUT that holds marketable securities). The balance of the required distribution first comes out of current-year capital gains, and then the rest of the distribution is funded by the initial sale of the asset, which is the deferred capital gain.

In the absence of a trust, the donor would recognize a massive capital gain up front. As mentioned in the previous section, this may put the person in the 20 percent capital gain bracket plus the 3.8 percent Obamacare surtax, plus state income tax. The CRUT smooths out the ride. The tax is paid more gradually, and if some of the pent-up gain remains after death, it isn't taxed at all.

But wait, there's more. The initial contribution also triggers a potential massive charitable deduction. Because the ultimate beneficiary is a charity, it is considered a current gift, but not the entire amount. In a somewhat convoluted calculation, the age of the person, the percentage distribution, and the interest rate are combined to come up with a present value of the ultimate gift. That present value is then taken as a charitable deduction. This is subject to the same 30 percent AGI limitation as discussed in the previous section. The icing on the cake is that the asset leaves the estate and is not counted for estate tax.

This all sounds wonderful, but what's the downside? First, the gift is irrevocable. You cannot take the assets back once given. Second, you have to at least take 5 percent as an income stream (which may not jive with your goals). Third, a qualified charity must at least wind up with a present value not less than 10 percent of the asset (so no setting the payout rate at 20 percent).

There are other variants of the CRUT. There is the CLAT (charitable lead annuity trust) where the charity gets the annual payments for your life and your beneficiaries keep the assets upon your passing. There is also a NIMCRUT (net income with makeup CRUT). Under this vehicle, you are only eligible to take the income from the asset. If the income does not reach the payout percentage, the difference is made up in later years when the income is sufficient. The NIMCRUT can be more complex, so be prepared for higher tax prep and accounting bills.

Qualified Accounts

Not all types of accounts are treated the same when you die. Assets not held inside of an IRA (stocks, bonds, real estate, partnership interests, etc.) have their basis stepped up to fair market value on the date of death. So the IBM stock you bought in the 1960s and never sold because the capital gain was too high can now be sold with little to no gain by your beneficiaries. Similarly, rental property completely depreciated with a similar capital gain situation can now be sold for no gain, or depreciation started at anew, with increased basis.

What does not get a step-up in basis is anything held inside of an IRA or annuity. This is important. A substantial percentage of people's net worth is tied up in tax-qualified accounts. During their lifetimes, they take money out and pay the tax. When an IRA is passed onto another individual (a child, mainly), that child will continue to pay the income tax based upon the child's tax rate. If the child dies, it goes to his or her beneficiaries, and then those new beneficiaries have required distributions and pay tax. At some point, the government gets its tax revenue.

This isn't all bad. The beneficiary is required to take required minimum distributions, but over their own lifetimes. A person in his or her seventies has to take around 4 percent out of his or her IRA every year. A person in their thirties starts taking around 2 percent. This may not seem like a lot, but for compounding purposes, it can be quite powerful. Like the previous owner's RMD, the beneficiary's percentage goes up over time, and often at a faster rate.

However, many of the clients that we work with feel like they are giving substantial enough sums to their kids and want to make a community impact. Charitable organizations know this, and more and more, they are pushing for legacy giving (gifts left after death). IRAs are great vehicles for legacy gifts, and as a matter of fact, my family has committed IRA money to a legacy campaign.

As noted in the CRUT section, qualified charities don't have an income tax problem. Because they are untaxed entities, they can recognize unlimited amounts of income and not have to worry about losing a substantial portion to the government.

Let's learn by example. Professor X is unmarried and has two children, Scott and Jean, both in the 28 percent federal tax bracket and 9 percent state bracket. Professor X has a $2 million IRA, a $10.5 million stock portfolio, and a house worth $500,000. He also has a keen interest in leaving some money to charity. His goal is to give $1 million to a qualified charity and the rest to his children. His first thought is to give the IRA to the kids:

Gross Estate:	$13 million
Charitable Deduction:	$1 million
Net Estate:	$12 million
Exemption (2018):	$11.4 million
Taxable Estate:	$600,000
Estate Tax (40%):	$240,000
Kids' Income Tax (assume: 37% of IRA):	$740,000

Net to Charity: $1 million

Net to Children: $11.02 million

Splitting $11 million between two people is not a bad deal, but in the above scenario, almost a quarter of a million dollars ends up going to the government. This irked Professor X, so he decided to leave the IRA to charity instead.

Gross Estate: $12 million

Charitable Deduction: $1 million

Net Estate: $12 million

Exemption: $11.4 million

Taxable Estate: $600,000

Estate Tax (40%): $240,000

Charity's Income Tax (0% of IRA): $0

Kids' Income Tax (37% of remaining IRA): $370,000

Net to Charity: $1 million

Net to Children: $11.39 million

By switching from which pocket he was giving to charity, Professor X's children netted an additional $370,000. Many reading this may say to themselves rather sarcastically, "I'm so glad his children, who were already getting $5.5 million each, are going to now get closer to $5.7 million." I get that sentiment. At the same time, I'd rather have the kids blow the money on a fancy car than give it to the government that'll waste it on an archaic program that nobody uses.

I'm sure many disagree, but by giving his IRA to charity, his dollar stretches more and passes to those he cares about most. Estate tax aside, even if we are talking about a smaller amount, and charity is part of the plan, more will go to the kids or grandkids if IRAs are used to fund charitable intentions.

Check, Please!

Nearly everyone can donate at least some small portion of their time or money to a cause or organization that's important to them. If you're in a position to give more, here are some points to keep in mind:

1. **Get your own estate in order first.** While having kids is usually the impetus for starting a plan, once you have assets to worry about, see an estate planning attorney.

2. **Charitable planning should be a component of a well-thought-out financial plan.** Older generations may have considered philanthropic endeavors to be an afterthought, but our generation should take more responsibility.

3. **We like to wait to make gifts to people and charity until we are dead, but that might not give us the most satisfaction.** Giving while you are alive lets you see the impact

you make and gives you leverage over institutions vying for your dollars.

4. **Be strategic about your giving.** Aside from cutting checks, there are ways to make gifts to charity such that you get to retain income and maximize savings on income tax.

5. **Don't forget about IRAs in your charitable planning.** By leaving these tax disadvantaged assets to charity, a decedent can avoid estate tax and the beneficiaries can avoid income tax.

Acknowledgements

I stand on the shoulders of many.

I first thank God for granting me life, sustaining me, and enabling me to reach this occasion.

I owe a huge debt of gratitude to my parents: my mother, Darcy Rubin, and my Father, Marvin Rubin. They worked long and hard to get me through my childhood. It's amazing that I made it through alive, let alone to the point where I wrote a book. I'm sure they had doubts about me along the way, but they never showed it. I'm sure they questioned their decisions, but never wavered. It is a testament to parental love that I have achieved all that I have.

My wife, Libby Werba, who has taken care of everything while I headed to work and wrote this book, is the unsung hero of the story. When clients ask me if my wife works, I always say, "She does, and a hell of a lot harder than I do." Taking care of three kids and a house is no small feat, the hours are long, and the pay is crappy.

Alan Werba has been my mentor for the greater part of a decade. When we first met fourteen years ago I had never given a thought about investing. His book "The Prudent Investor's Guide to Beating the Market," is one of the top five most influential books in my life.

When we started working together in 2009, he gave me space to explore what it is to be a financial advisor, helped me buy a practice, and has had sound advice all along the way. I'm sure that I have driven him crazy over the last decade, but he never let it get to him (as far as I can tell).

The reason I get up in the morning is for my children. I get to see them almost every morning when I wake up, nearly every night when they go to bed, and I wouldn't trade it for the world. Their curiosity inspires me, and at times infuriates me. They challenge me to be a better person. Sometimes I fail, occasionally succeed, but I always try to do my best.

An enormous shout out to Loring Ward International, who provided all data and graphics used in this book. They have been amazing business partners since I started. The resources they provide are unmatched, and *Financial Adulting* would not have been possible without them.

There were many people who edited this book before I published it (believe it or not).

My eternal thanks goes out to Panteha Healey. When I asked my group of friends and business colleagues to review the first draft, almost nobody answered the bell. Prior to the book, I had only spoken with Panteha a couple of times, but she spent more time and energy on this book than anyone else besides me. The funny, snarky, and quick-witted lines in the book are almost entirely due to her. She is a talented writer, a kind person, and I am blessed to have worked with her.

Chrissy Guthrie was also instrumental in the editing process. I look back at the first rough draft I sent her and cringe (yes, this book was even worse at one point). She stuck with it, and did the first content edit, and then copy editing.

My classmate and fellow Stevenson Statesman editor Caryn Sandler Strean did the line editing on the book. Never shy to point out her disagreements with my writing, I appreciate her hard work.

I also had a number of readers that helped on various sections.

Grant DiCianni, whom I met on a cold rainy soccer field when I was four years old, supported me throughout the process. His friendship over the last thirty-five plus years has sustained me at some of my lowest points, and I am grateful to have him as a hetero-life mate.

Mike Morales reviewed "Between Death and Taxes, Choose Death." This was no small feat since the new Tax Cuts and Jobs Act had just come out. I needed a real expert to come in and do a thorough reading, and Mike stepped up and brought his substantial expertise to the table.

Tim Rembowski read through "Insurance: The Only Path to Hakuna Matata." I've known Tim several years professionally, and knew he'd have some great insights into a complicated subject matter. He did not let me down. He helped beef up and clarify sections of that chapter.

Thomas L. Pencek and Laura Testa-Reyes helped put the finishing touches on *Financial Adulting*, and put enough polish on it that the book actually looks good. I know I needed the pros to go the final stretch, and Tom and Laura were a no-brainer.

My newest partner, Jason Papier, did the compliance review on the book. Thank the Lord I am not in charge of compliance. It's an awful job, but Jason performs dutifully, and keeps me from running afoul of the SEC.

About the Author

Aaron Rubin
JD, CPA, CFP®

Aaron Rubin brings a broad background to his client experience. From financial planning to estate and tax planning, Aaron advises on the most important parts of his clients' lives from planning exits from businesses to helping widows and divorcees regain the confidence they deserve. He takes particular pride in helping his young tech clients make tax savvy, financially sound decisions about their stock compensation packages.

He received his BA degree in Economics-Accounting-Spanish from Claremont McKenna College. He graduated cum laude from the University of Illinois College of Law and was admitted as a member of the California Bar in 2006. He is licensed as a certified public accountant, and has also obtained licensing as a life, health and property and casualty insurance agent in the state of California. In 2009, Aaron also received his CFP® designation.

Aaron started his career in accounting, working at Deloitte (an international CPA firm), where he focused on high net worth individual income tax returns. He then moved on to Abbott Stringham & Lynch (a local CPA firm) expanding his focus to estate and gift tax returns and planning.

When not helping clients plan, Aaron dedicates his time to not-for-profits. He has been a board member of Congregation Beth Emek in the past and is currently on their legacy giving campaign.

He and his wife Libby live in the Bay Area with their three daughters Natalie, Gwen, and Emmy. Not to mention their Goldendoodle, Mollie.